439

The
Sophisticated
Poll Watcher's
Guide

George Gallup

PRINCETON OPINION PRESS

Dedicated to the daily newspapers of America whose publishers and editors saw the opportunities in this new field of journalism and whose financial support has made possible our forty years of public opinion research into the social, political, and economic problems of the nation.

Composed and printed by Science Press,
Ephrata, Pennsylvania 17522

Foreword

This guidebook has been written to answer the questions of those individuals who have occasion to use, interpret, explain, or challenge poll findings. The questions come from newspaper and television commentators, magazine editors, U.S. senators and governors, members of the state and national political committees, and political science professors.

Each was asked to list the aspects of polling that need further explanation or clarification. The response to this request was immediate and great—ample evidence of the confusion that exists in respect to polling methods and practices and the place of this field of research in democratic societies.

This book attempts to answer in a full and frank manner all the questions raised. An effort has been made to follow the suggestion made by many—to explain the methods and procedures employed in survey work in language that a layman can understand. Technical terms, therefore, have been avoided whenever possible.

The questions asked are included in the text, and in all but a few instances, in the exact language in which they were stated. In a few instances minor changes have been made in the interest of clarification. Some questions have had to be omitted because of their technical nature.

While most of the basic points about polling and survey methods are covered by the questions received, obviously some have been overlooked. For this reason, this book has been planned to cover, in future editions, any points that may not have been included, or new points that may arise in the months ahead.

Many excellent books on polls and public opinion have appeared in the last three decades. A selection of these will be found in the bibliography in the appendix of this book. The reader who wishes to delve more deeply into research procedures, especially the more technical aspects, is urged to make use of this bibliography.

Books in the field of public opinion fall into three broad categories: those concerned with the nature of public opinion, those dealing with survey methods and statistical procedures, and those which describe and interpret poll findings. In this latter category are three books dealing chiefly with Gallup Poll findings.

The first book, appearing in 1940, *The Pulse of Democracy*, was written by George Gallup and Saul Forbes Rae. In 1946, William Lydgate wrote *What our People Think*. The third, covering the post-war period, 1946 to 1960, was written by John M. Fenton, under the title *In Your Opinion*.

A set of reference books, published in 1972, provides a digest of the findings of every poll released since the Gallup Poll was established in 1935. The three-volume reference work has been compiled and published by Random House.

The writer wishes to pay special tribute to Paul K.

Perry, who has been responsible for the development of the polling methods and statistical procedures used in the survey work undertaken by the American Institute of Public Opinion, more commonly known as the Gallup Poll.

Many individuals share the credit for the worldwide acceptance of survey methods in the field of public opinion. Among these are Hadley Cantril, Claude Robinson, and Elmo Roper. Others who have made important contributions are Archibald Crossley, Paul Lazarsfeld, Rensis Likert, Angus Campbell, and Louis Harris. The survey research centers at Michigan, Chicago, and Columbia Universities have added substantially to the stature of this new field of research.

Some of the very best work in gauging public opinion is being done by state polls, the Minnesota, California, Iowa, Michigan, and Texas polls, to cite five of the best known.

Survey work abroad meets the highest standards in most nations; in fact, public opinion is being assessed and reported on a regular basis in every important nation of the Free World.

The Roper Public Opinion Center at Williams College serves as a repository for much of the public opinion data now being collected throughout the world. Most of the survey findings of the Gallup Poll in the United States, and many of the poll results of its affiliates in other parts of the world, are available at this center, to scholars and others who wish access to poll findings.

The Public Opinion Quarterly, official publication

of the American Association for Public Opinion Research, has, since 1937 when it was founded, recorded progress and developments in this field of study.

Finally, the writer wishes to thank all of the commentators, editors, and public officials who took the time to write out the questions to which they would like answers and, in many instances, to offer their views about polling and its place in the democratic process. Their names are listed, alphabetically, below:

Robert S. Allen
Senator Gordon Allott
William D. Altus
Robert C. Angell
Mrs. Tobin Armstrong
Sidney Ascher
Kenneth Auchincloss
A. T. Baker
A. Doak Barnett
Mrs. Harold Barton
Lucille Beachy
Senator Wallace F. Bennett
Evelyn M. Berger
Lee Berton
Robert Bierstedt
Guthrie S. Birkhead
Robert C. Birney
Joseph B. Board, Jr.
Jean Boese
Richard Boeth
Emory S. Bogardus
Edward S. Bordin
Harold Borko
Raymond V. Bowers
Mrs. Forrest Braden
Senator William E. Brock

David S. Broder
Senator Edward W. Brooke
Art Buchwald
Governor John A. Burns
Governor William T. Cahill
Angus Campbell
Leslie Carpenter
John B. Carroll
Raymond Carroll
Mrs. John A. Cauble
William Chapman
Marquis Childs
Carroll D. Clark
Matt Clark
Thomas I. Cook
Brownlee Sands Corrin
Leonars S. Cottrell, Jr.
Gardner Cowles
Meredith P. Crawford
Walter Cronkite
Randolph Crossley
Joe Crump
Ernest Cutts
Governor Deane C. Davis
Sid Davis
Nicholas J. Demerath

Governor John Dempsey
Richard Doan
John T. Doby
Senator Robert J. Dole
Leonard W. Doob
Mayor Joseph A. Doorley, Jr.
Paul F. Douglass
Dan Dowling
Geoffrey Drummond
Roscoe Drummond
Mel Elfin
Douglas G. Ellson
Amitai Etzioni
Mayor Charles Evers
Senator Paul J. Fannin
Jules Feiffer
Leonard W. Ferguson
Thomas Foley
Timothy Foote
Thomas R. Ford
Roy G. Francis
Wes Gallagher
David B. Gardner
Murray J. Gart
J. A. Gengerelli
Gino Germani
Jack W. Germond
Jacob W. Getzels
Mrs. M. Stanley Ginn
Sidney Goldstein
Senator Barry Goldwater
Harrison G. Gough
Governor William L. Guy
George H. Ingram
Jerry Hannifin
Thomas Harper
Paul Harvey
Governor Linwood Holton

Senator Harold E. Hughes
Senator Hubert H. Humphrey
Mrs. Lucie Humphrey
Edward G. Janeway
Leon Jaroff
Senator Jacob K. Javits
Robert E. Kennedy
John H. Kerr
Peter Kihss
James J. Kilpatrick
John S. Knight
Governor Warren P. Knowles
Joseph Kraft
Victor Lasky
David Lawrence
John E. Leard
Vince Leonard
Max Lerner
Carl P. Leubsdorf
Paul F. Levy
Flora Lewis
Governor Frank Licht
Mrs. Russell T. Lund
Robert J. Markle
Everett G. Martin
Senator Charles McC.
   Mathias, Jr.
Senator John L. McClellan
Albert W. McCollough
Mrs. Hope McCormick
Donald McLean
Senator Lee Metcalf
Karl E. Meyer
Edwin G. Middleton
Norman C. Miller
Thomas Z. Minehart

Senator Joseph M. Montoya
Mrs. Collis P. Moore
Edward P. Morgan
Clem Morgello
Senator Frank E. Moss
Mrs. K. K. Neuberger
Edwin Newman
Tom Nicholson
Crosby Noyes
Mike O'Connor
Governor Richard B. Ogilvie
Murray Olderman
Dr. Mildred Otenasek
Senator Claiborne Pell
Senator Charles H. Percy
James M. Perry
Governor Russell W. Peterson
Governor Robert D. Ray
Thomas C. Reed
Mrs. Eleanor R. Ring
J. D. Roberts
Governor Nelson A.
    Rockefeller
Bill Roeder
Robert Roth
Senator William V. Roth
Walter Rundle
Bill Ryan

Morrie Ryskind
Martin Schram
Lloyd Shearer
Hugh Sidey
Senator Margaret Chase Smith
Senator John Sparkman
Mrs. Keith Spurrier
Mrs. Jack L. Stacy
Sarah Ann Stauffer
John L. Steele
Rafael Steinberg
Senator Adlai Stevenson III
Sherman E. Stock
Richard B. Stoner
Brian Sullivan
Robert D. Stuart, Jr.
Senator John C. Tower
Walter Trohan
Mrs. Frank Wallner
Senator Lowell P. Weicker, Jr.
William S. White
Mrs. Alice Wilder
Jules Witcover
Tom Wicker
Whitney M. Young, Jr.
Marvin Zim
Paul D. Zimmerman

GEORGE GALLUP

Table of Contents

xi

Section 1
POLLS—WHAT PURPOSE
DO THEY SERVE?

Public Opinion Polls and Leadership
Polls and the Electoral Process
The Bandwagon Myth

Public Opinion Polls and Leadership

"Leadership by polls is weak, uninspired, un-informed, not innovative, and contributes only to temporary success. There is a tendency for politicians or elected officials to tell the people what the polls show and the public wants to hear."

These are strong words, voiced by the governor of a midwestern state.

Before the matter of polls and leadership can be discussed intelligently, it is necessary to point out a commonly held misconception that arises from the failure to differentiate between the measuring device, represented by polls, and what is measured.

Polling is merely an instrument for gauging public opinion. When a president, or any other leader, pays attention to poll results, he is, in effect, paying attention to the views of the people. Any other interpretation is nonsense. One might as well insist that a thermometer makes the weather, or that a microscope should be held accountable for the bacteria its lens reveals.

The basic question, therefore, is not whether the leader is paying too much attention to polls, but whether he is paying too much attention to the views of the people.

It is not incumbent upon a leader, even in a democracy, to follow the wishes of the people slavishly. But the very nature of democracy makes it imperative that public opinion be taken into account in reaching decisions about legislative goals.

The final responsibility for decisions rests, obviously, with the leader. He must be guided by his own best judgment, and conscience, as Winston Churchill once said:

> "Nothing is more dangerous than to live in the temperamental atmosphere of a Gallup Poll, always taking one's temperature . . . There is only one duty, only one safe course, and that is to try to be right and not fear to do or say what you believe to be right."

No one is likely to quarrel with this statement of Churchill. Every citizen wants the head of his nation to do the "right" thing; but all too often the "right" thing usually turns out to be what the particular leader thinks is right.

The image of the strong leader who brooks no opposition and who pursues relentlessly his ideas of what is "right" unfortunately fits such malodorous characters of recent decades as Hitler, Mussolini, and Stalin. All of them were guided by a deep-seated conviction that their policies were "right" for their people. Hitler scoffed at the "foolish masses" and spoke of the "granite stupidity of mankind." He felt no compulsion for taking account of the views of the people because they were mere "ballot cattle." Mussolini insisted that Fascism had "thrown on the dump heap" the "lifeless theories" of democracy which he once described as a "stinking corpse." Stalin had even less respect for the people. He dealt with all opposition in a simple way—by slaughtering millions of those whom he suspected.

The point at issue is not whether public opinion should be completely ignored, or blindly followed. The question is *when* to take account of the public's views, and the *degree of importance* that should be attached to these opinions.

It may be possible for historians at the end of this century to test the accuracy of an observation once made by Theodore Roosevelt. He said:

"Day in and day out the plain people of this country will make fewer mistakes in governing themselves than any smaller group of men will make in trying to govern them."

At the close of World War I, Colonel Edward M. House, close adviser to Woodrow Wilson, expressed this view:

"I have come to the conclusion that the consensus of public opinion comes nearer being right than the opinions of the leaders of the country. Only now and then do you find a leader who sees more clearly than the people in the aggregate."

Some years later, during the national crisis that engulfed the United States in the first year of World War II, Dr. Robert Millikan, then president of the

California Institute of Technology, after reviewing the findings of polls for that period, made this statement in a public address:

> "One may be discouraged about the administration, about Congress, about the Supreme Court, about the racketeering of labor leadership, about political corruption, about many ominous tendencies in American life, but he cannot be discouraged about the way the common man seems to be understanding and correctly appraising, on the average, the American situation . . . If all of this does not show the average American has more intelligence and more conscience than his political leaders, then I don't know straight thinking and straight social morals when I see them."

If Robert Millikan were alive today, he would have more evidence to support his conclusion that the American people have judged the issues of recent years more wisely than their leaders. While this conclusion comes from a prejudiced witness, the record of the public's views on all the important issues of the last 40 years is now part of the record that anyone can examine.

The Pentagon Papers have revealed how easy it is for leaders to make wrong judgments when surrounded by intimates who think the same way, and when the public is not aware of the nature of the problem, and has no opportunity to question or to debate policies under consideration.

It is easy for a leader to make the decision to keep

secret the details of many problems, particularly those in the area of foreign policy, under the honest conviction that he can deal with the situation better himself. But this ignores the people's "right to know" especially when it is their lives and pocketbooks that are involved.

In this discussion about the people and their leaders, it is relevant to point out that the nation which is regarded as the best governed in the entire world today[1] is a nation that gives more weight to public opinion—and less to leaders—than any other nation of the world. That country is Switzerland.

Although it is a small country in population and in area, problems are much the same as those met in every democracy. In one respect the country has more. Three different languages are spoken and all are legal. A fourth, Romansch, is also spoken in one area. The twenty-two cantons all have their own special history, customs, and way of life.

By means of the referendum, Switzerland gives its citizens the opportunity to voice their opinions on every major issue. One might say that the nation is run by a census-type poll of the electorate. Government services are headed by competent persons, but charismatic leaders of the kind found in other nations are virtually non-existent.

Switzerland has been able to keep out of wars. Its standard of living is one of the highest in the world. No general strikes have been called since 1935, and

---

[1] Poll of International Leaders, 1970.

still labor is well paid. Taxes are moderate. The crime rate is low. The schools are good. The circulation of daily newspapers, on a per capita basis, is the highest in the world. The people do not vote themselves low taxes or large benefits. They are responsible citizens who run their country in the best tradition.

No purpose is served in trying to prove or disprove the hypothesis that people are better able to govern themselves than their leaders. This discussion, to be constructive, must deal with ways in which the insights and the collective wisdom of both leaders and the people can be fully utilized.

One observation that experience would seem to support comes from James Bryce, the world's great authority on the workings of democracy, who said:

"The people who are the power entitled to say what they want are less qualified to say how, and in what form, they are to obtain it; or, in other words, public opinion can determine ends, but it is less fit to examine and select means to those ends."

The record of the public's views on scores of issues that have arisen in recent years should convince the most hardened skeptic that the collective judgment of the people is amazingly sound, even in the complex area of foreign policy. In fact, it is in the area of foreign policy that polls can be particularly useful to leadership. Survey results can reveal the kind and level of information which the public has in respect to a given policy and the nature of the opposition likely to be encountered. Failure to take account of the public's views can spell disaster for the policy, and defeat for the leader who, regardless of the merit of his program, must still account to the electorate for his actions at the next election.

Without polls and therefore without adequate knowledge of the views of the people, a leader is in the hapless position of a military commander who must go into battle without knowing the strength or the deployment of the enemy troops he faces. If, through negligence or lack of understanding, he fails to obtain this kind of intelligence, he courts defeat. By the same token, the civil leader who attempts to carry out a program without bothering to learn all he can about public opinion is equally derelict.

A sane middle course is suggested by Harold Wilson. Writing in the Britannica Book of the Year only a few months after his predicted success in June, 1970, the ex-Prime Minister of Great Britain made these comments, perhaps the most sagacious that have come from any leader in public life about polls:

"The statesman's conclusions, then, might be: Accord to the polls interest, but not idolatry. Seek not to ban their publication, whether on election eve or at any other time. Regard them as an honest attempt to record the state of public opinion, at one moment in time, on one issue of political importance; or, less reliably, as an assessment not of opinion but of that indefinable phenomenon, the public mood on the broad political situation—a factor in, not a determinant of, policy. Scrutinize the form of the question and the detail of the answer. Insist that publication of the results be frank and fair, not influenced—whether in selection, omission, or slant—by the editorial or proprietorial prejudices of those who control publication, for public opinion polls constitute a public service. And service means they should be a servant, not a purported master, of the process of democratic decision making.

"Treat them, then with respect, as you would give to any honest and expert professional assessment of facts that you have to take into account. And then recognize that you were elected, as legislator, as an executive, to exercise a judgment—not on what is expedient, or electorally rewarding, but a judgment on what is right."

Time is required for every new institution—such as that represented by modern public opinion polls—to find its proper place and its greatest usefulness. Meanwhile, some critics are wont to claim that the institution serves no purpose or is actually perverting other institutions.

One of the editors of a newsmagazine makes this point:

"Polls are no longer necessary in public affairs because communications are so vastly expanded . . . one imagines that depending on

*them has helped destroy real political leader-
ship."*

True, communications have improved at an amazing rate. Today the ordinary citizen who is willing
to spend three or four hours a day reading newspapers, magazines, and books can be as well informed
about current affairs as the typical congressman.

To be most effective democracy requires an informed electorate. But it also depends upon another
type of communication, the communication of the
views and wishes of the people to elected officials. Unless the public actively participates in the democratic
process, nothing much is gained by being well informed.

James Bryce, writing some eighty years ago, long
before the advent of the modern public opinion poll,
made this observation:

"The obvious weakness of government by
public opinion is the difficulty of ascertaining
it."

Bryce was so certain of this that he predicted that
the next and final stage in the development of democracies would be reached when the will of the people
could be known at all times and without the need of
"election machinery."

The public opinion poll supplies this machinery,
not perfectly, but certainly better than any other
means.

One of the greatest services that the modern poll

can and does perform is to give elected officials some idea of the views of the "inarticulate majority." Without this knowledge, legislators are constantly in danger of confusing minority with majority opinion.

Pressure groups in the past, and even today, take advantage of this situation. In fact, virtually every large special-interest group in the nation has its own paid lobbyists in Washington to influence legislation that affects them directly or indirectly.

Some of the work of lobbyists is useful but all too often they resort to two devices in their attempt to influence legislators and legislation. They may offer a handsome contribution to the congressman's next election campaign if he goes along with their demands . . . nothing but a form of bribery. More often they try to impress the congressman with a claim that they represent a large block of voters who will punish him by voting against him at the next election if he does not accede to their wishes.

Professor Thomas A. Bailey, author of *The Man in the Street*, has summed up this latter effort on the part of lobbyists in these words:

> "The 'pressure boys' have perfected techniques for making noise all out of proportion to the numbers of their constituents, and in so doing, they provide another example of the "tyranny of the minority.' Clever operatives can stir up a tremendous pother, particularly when they assail their congressman with padded petitions, 'parrot' letters, and form telegrams signed with names lifted from the telephone directory.

"The nervous legislator, ever anxious for his seat, may easily be misled by the aggressive minority that deluges him with telegrams, while the great and apathetic majority tends to its daily diversions. He may be unduly impressed when a man whom he has never heard of appears as the alleged spokesman for 22,-000,000 people. The congressman in such circumstances would do well to remember the three tailors of Tooley Street, who, in addressing a petition to the king, began, 'We, the people of England . . .'."

Without benefit of polls there can be no clear indication of the public's wishes to refute the claims of pressure groups. Minorities, especially when large financial interests are at stake, can be effectively organized; majorities are impossible to organize for the purpose of influencing legislation. Their views can be known only through the medium of the modern poll.

One of many examples that could be cited to show how poll results can explode the claims of pressure groups has to do with the gun lobby, certainly one of the most effective pressure groups ever to appear on the American legislative scene. This group has fought every law proposed in any state or in Congress that would restrict in any way the sale of guns and ammunition.

Because this pressure group, headed by the National Rifle Association and amply supported by makers and importers of guns and ammunition, has been so successful in stopping legislation, the United

States stands alone among the major nations of the world in its lack of control over the sale and distribution of guns of all types—from revolvers to machine guns.

As early as 1938, the Gallup Poll found that more than seventy per cent of all Americans polled on the issue favored laws to curb the sale of hand guns. In later polls large majorities supported laws that would require all guns to be registered, as they must be in virtually every developed nation.

Despite these views of the majority of the nation's citizens, the gun lobby has been so effective in its pressure tactics that most congressmen are afraid to vote in favor of any legislation contrary to the wishes of this powerful and aggressive group.

One of the reasons for its effectiveness is that a small army of people can be alerted on short notice to write letters to their legislators, or call upon them personally, or fill hearing rooms when legislation on this issue is being discussed.

After the publication of survey results showing the public's desire to enact stricter gun control laws, the office of the Gallup Poll was deluged with letters from all parts of the nation—all inspired by the central agency. Many not only protested, in language dictated by the lobby, but contained threats against the polling organization and those who headed it.

Often it is assumed that Congress reflects accurately the views and wishes of the people. And the reason advanced is that members of this body, and especially of the House of Representatives, must be sensitive to the will of the people since they have to face the voters every two years.

This is a naive viewpoint, which fails to take account of modern-day realities. Except in tightly contested districts, congressmen need pay little attention to majority opinion on any given issue. While it is theoretically possible to defeat a member of Congress, he will, in the course of a two-year term, have voted on scores of bills, some that the people favor and some that they do not. And few voters, except in very unusual circumstances, will even know where their congressman stood on a given issue.

The assumption that Congress does reflect accurately the will of the majority on given issues and is, therefore, a good barometer of opinion on these issues, has led many individuals astray. Even those who are expert in matters of government are prone to equate Congressional action with public opinion under the mistaken notion that Congress is a perfect mirror of public opinion. Walter Lippmann in his book, *The Public Philosophy*, falls into this serious error.

Few writers of recent decades have had the insight into our national and international problems or have written about them with greater clarity and intelligence. Yet, Mr. Lippmann fails to make the distinction between the public's views on many of the great issues of recent years and the actions taken by Congress.

Lippmann writes:

"Mass opinion has acquired mounting power

in this country. It has shown itself to be a dangerous master of decisions when the stakes are life and death. The unhappy truth is that the prevailing public opinion has been destructively wrong at the critical junctures. They have compelled the governments, which usually know what would have been wiser, or was necessary, or was more expedient, to be too late with too little, or too long with too much, too pacifist in peace and too bellicose in war, too neutralist or appeasing in negotiation or too intransigent. When the world wars came the people . . . could not be aroused to the exertions and sacrifices of the struggle until they had been incited to passionate hatred, and had become intoxicated with unlimited hope."

If Mr. Lippmann had consulted the record, he would have discovered that on almost every single one of these points, the public took an entirely different viewpoint from Congress, and in many instances, the nation's leadership. It was the legislators—not the public—who were guilty of the shortsightedness pointed out by Lippmann. The record since Lippmann wrote *The Public Philosophy* supplies even more evidence on this point.

In fact, poll results have on many critical occasions given congressmen the courage they would otherwise not have had to vote for what they assumed to be unpopular measures.

One of many cases in point is the draft law enacted in 1940. Survey results showed the nation favored enacting peace-time conscription by a sizeable majority. But Congress, even after the start of World War II, under pressure from letter writers and the isolationist bloc adopted the measure by a single vote. Without poll results showing the exact opposite of the views expressed by letter writers, Congress would undoubtedly have defeated this legislation.

Virtually every measure during the World War II period—repeal of the neutrality act, the destroyers-for-bases deal, wage-price controls, higher taxes to meet war costs, total manpower conscription, curbing strikes in war industries, and many other measures for conducting the war more vigorously—was favored by the majority of people long before Congress passed, or in some instances, defeated these measures. Even in the matter of bringing the troops home immediately after the war, it was Congress, not the people, who insisted on hurrying up the process.

Two decades before the Watergate scandal, the American public favored basic reforms in the electoral process, including strict limits on election campaign spending. A majority has favored changing radically the way campaigns are conducted, making them more informative and meaningful and less given to trivia and mud-slinging. Had the limitations on campaign spending, favored by the public, been adopted, Watergate would likely have never occurred.

These are but a few of scores of examples that might be cited to show that contrary to "destroying real political leadership" public opinion polls have provided the very basis for courageous political leadership.

A political scientist on the faculty of an Eastern college asks this question:

"Are polls really necessary when we have elections every two years or oftener to show what the people are thinking?"

While elections may reveal the general direction that the majority of voters wish governing bodies to take, they are typically a poor, and often a misleading guide, to specific legislation.

Bryce answered this question in this manner:

"At elections, it is for a candidate that votes are given, and as his personality or his local influence may count for more than his principles, the choice of one man against another is an imperfect way of expressing the mind of of a constituency."

The temptation to interpret election returns as expressions of majority opinion on issues has led to many serious errors in this century. In the presidential election of 1920 Warren G. Harding defeated the Democrat, James Cox, by an impressive margin. After the election, Harding concluded that his victory represented a mandate from the people to stay out of the League of Nations. All facts gathered since indicate that if the voters had been given the opportunity to vote on this issue in a separate referendum, the vote would have favored joining the League by more than 60 per cent.

In 1928 Herbert Hoover scored a great popular vote victory over Al Smith. Hoover read into the election figures a desire on the part of the American public to continue the prohibition experiment. Yet again, if the voters had been given the opportunity to record their views on the question of repeal or modification of the prohibition amendment, a sizeable majority would have voted for modification. When given this chance a few years later, in 1933, they voted for outright repeal of the 18th amendment by the very great majority of 70 per cent to 30 per cent.

President Franklin Roosevelt and his advisors pointed to his great victory in the 1936 election as proof of a mandate to enlarge the Supreme Court. By this time modern polls had come into being and the views of the people could be determined on this one issue alone, separated from the many issues that typically enter into every presidential election. On two occasions before and after the 1936 election, the Gallup Poll had tested sentiment on the Supreme Court. Both times a clear majority had voted against curbing its powers, even though a large majority of voters had voted for Roosevelt. When the fight ended and President Roosevelt had given up his plan, virtually the same proportion opposed the idea as had opposed it earlier, before the fight had been carried to the people.

Professor Bailey has summed up the situation this way:

"To assert that a clear referendum can emerge from the confused and dustfilled arena of a national election is to fly in the face of reason. Yet the leatherlunged politician, after he has won, claims a mandate on everything in sight. Sometimes he claims a mandate on issues that were mentioned only incidentally, or that were not mentioned at all . . . but he can invariably outshout the defeated, for the defeated, like the absent, are always wrong.

"We try to operate under a crazy system. We hold elections, and then try to guess what they mean which is a thoroughly unscientific procedure. Until such time as we are willing to have true referenda on specific issues, we shall have to seek the truth not in official election returns but in unofficial public opinion polls. While the latter admittedly have their limitations, they are applied science in its purest form when compared with the present kind of guesswork."

It will be many years—perhaps decades—before election machinery can be changed to permit voters to register their views on specific issues at the same time they vote on candidates. Only simple reforms would have to be instituted to permit this, but the cultural lag—the difficulty in making even simple changes in election procedures—is so great that official referenda are something for the distant future.

Polls and the Electoral Process

Many of the doubts about the value of public opinion polls spring from the belief that polls not only report but influence opinion, especially during election campaigns.

One of the nation's leading senators, representing an Eastern state, has this question:

"Is there a danger that polls have become a dangerous element in our electoral process in recent years, influencing elections rather than offering insights into voter sentiment on candidates and issues?"

To answer this question in a meaningful way, it is essential to establish a few facts about the electoral process. Only by doing this will it be possible to see whether modern polls constitute a "dangerous element" or whether they are helping to improve a process that is in vital need of improvement.

The Constitution, contrary to a widely held belief, does not specify the manner in which candidates are to be selected and elected to federal office. The Founding Fathers assumed that outstanding men would seek public office, even at great personal sacrifice. The introduction of the party system, which

George Washington hoped would never occur, brought a new kind of person into politics—the professional or career politician. And the professional clings to his patronage, and to all the other election practices—no matter how indefensible—that have operated to help elect him to office and add to his powers.

Nothing in American political life is so urgently needed as reform in the practices of selecting and electing candidates. But important reform is probably many decades off. Meanwhile, public opinion polls can help to remedy some of the more obvious weaknesses.

Senator Joseph Clark, in his book, *Congress, the Sapless Branch*, points out that to understand Congress it is crucial to recognize that many members of the House and Senate are elected permanently when they are elected once. They can thus:

"afford to be indifferent to all but the most major national political currents."

Most laymen, and even students of government, for that matter, overlook the fact that nomination in a primary election, rather than the November general election, is the really meaningful part of the electoral process because of the preponderance of one-party districts.

In Senator Clark's words:

"Our two-party system, like our private enterprise system, is supposed to have competition as its foundation . . . this conception of electoral competition is crucial in a free society. Politics... ought ideally to involve an *intra* party struggle for nomination, and an *inter* party struggle for election... Essentially, one-party politics is issueless politics. If the incumbent is renominated without a real contest and the general election is a formality, there is no need to campaign or to discuss issues. The dominant party candidate wins in a walk and holds his seat until he dies, quits, or is removed because he 'bucked the organization.'

"Patronage serves to create and nourish a political organization that is indifferent to public policy and therefore essentially amoral. By relying on tangible economic rewards to create a corps of the faithful large enough to produce victory at the polls, the machine extorts tribute from government, subordinates issues and debases the political process. In doing so it discourages able people from political participation and nurtures self-perpetuating cliques of political leaders unrepresentative of the governmental talent our country is capable of producing."

Congressman Richard Bolling in *House Out of Order* expresses similar views about the shortcomings of Congress. He, too, has little hope that Congress will reform itself. The impetus for change, he asserts, must come from outside pressures and will require the active concern of the American people.

The present system of primaries and conventions

was devised by party politicians and it is unlikely to be changed because it leaves the power of selection largely in their hands. Ordinary voters—the rank and file of the major parties—have little to say about the selection of candidates at the city, state, or national level. In theory they could—and in extreme cases do—revolt and name their own candidates but in practice the machine—which means one or just a few self-appointed persons—actually make the choice in a manner to serve their own purposes, not the good of the city, the state, or the nation. It is always possible for an outsider to throw his hat into the ring, but in most states he is certain to be crushed in the primaries by the machine.

A national committeewoman from a midwestern state adds this comment and plea:

> *"As a national committeewoman I deplore the fact that such a large percentage of the electorate are willing to allow political parties to choose candidates in a primary and to await the general election and then make a choice between candidates. They fail to exercise their franchise in a primary election when their choice could really be important."*

The most intelligent and far-reaching proposals— one might even add, the most revolutionary—for changing the electoral process and the composition of Congress come from a person who would never be described as a radical—Dwight D. Eisenhower.

In his book, *Waging Peace*, he proposes that senators be limited to two terms, or a total of twelve years.[1] He would also impose a twelve year limitation on members of the House, or a total of three terms of four years each. President Eisenhower states his case in these words:

"If the terms of the House members were extended to four years with tenure limited to three elections . . . and that of senators to two terms of six years . . . each man so serving would tend to think of his congressional career as an important and exciting interlude in his life, a period dedicated to the entire public rather than as a way of making a living or making a career of exercising continuous political power. Possibly each would spend less time in keeping his eyes on the next election and more in centering them on the good of the nation. A more rapid turn-over of the membership in both houses with its constant infusion of new blood would largely eliminate the 'career' politician in Congress, but I see little damage that would result from such a change except possibly to the personal ambitions of particular individuals.

"Many argue for the value of long experience

---

[1] President Harry S. Truman also proposed a two-term limit for Senators.

in Congress. Admittedly, experience may produce a greater skill in political maneuvering in the legislative process but (such experience) does not necessarily produce better statesmen."

President Eisenhower argues that one other important advantage of such a plan is that it would go far toward solving the problem of committee chairmanships in Congress which are chiefly filled on the basis of seniority. This system has produced a government within a government, a kind of oligarchy that Eisenhower's proposal would end.

Mr. Eisenhower was realistic enough, however, to recognize that an amendment to the Constitution to limit the term of office of both senators and representatives would never receive the blessing of Congress. And in this he is in accord with Senator Clark and Congressman Bolling.

The impetus for such a change will have to come from the people. It is worth noting that the American people have approved the Eisenhower plan for limiting the terms of office of senators and representatives in public opinion surveys dealing with this proposal.

Mr. Eisenhower also advocated a nationwide primary to be held on a given date in all states. All candidates for the Republican nomination would be voted on by rank and file members of the party, while members of the Democratic party recorded their candidate preferences in a like primary, on the same day.

A nationwide presidential primary, with all candidates listed, would overcome most of the weaknesses of the present system. In the states that presently do hold primaries, entering or not entering is a decision left to the candidate. Hubert Humphrey in the 1968 race never bothered to enter any of the open primaries and yet became the party's nominee.

Relatively few voters take the trouble to vote in states where primaries are held and largely because of this, the political machine can almost always produce enough support to elect its slate of candidates.

In the presidential campaign of 1964, Senator Goldwater fared badly in the primaries, and was not the first choice of the rank and file of the party at the time of the nominating convention. Nevertheless, he won the nomination.

> The right of the people to elect must embrace
> the right to select. Otherwise the whole pro-
> cess is a travesty.

While a nationwide primary is probably many years away, the public opinion poll can provide at least the same kind of results as a primary of this type. Public opinion surveys can establish which one of many candidates is most favored by the voters, and it can narrow the field to any two. This is important since five candidates representing the liberal (or conservative) wing of the party who oppose one conservative (or liberal) would split the vote five ways, giving the opposing candidate an unwarranted advantage.

This, of course, can be corrected in a manner, by a run-off election. But a second national primary election would have to be held unless a candidate emerged with at least 50 per cent in the first election.

The public opinion poll can perform another important service. In addition to finding out which of the candidates is preferred by the rank and file, it can, by means of "trial heats," pit one candidate against any opponent on the other side.

While the party convention probably should be in a position to make the final judgment as to candidates, certainly convention delegates owe it to their party to nominate the strongest presidential candidate, other things being equal.

The Republican convention of 1964 ignored poll findings regarding the strength of candidates. The candidate selected not only lost by one of the largest margins in this century, but in losing carried to defeat a number of candidates for the Senate and House from his own party. The great party imbalance of the years 1965 and 1966 was, in this sense, created by this failure to follow the views of the rank and file of the Republican party.

Eisenhower had other suggestions for changing the electoral process. He would change the way political conventions are run to introduce some semblance of decorum; he would advance the time of elections from November to September with inauguration of the new president in November—a change that would provide more time for the newly elected president to prepare his recommendations to Congress for the coming year. He would shorten the length of presidential campaigns. He would require each radio and television station to give six half-hours of prime time to permit each major party candidate an opportunity to present his case.

Most of these proposals have been put to the American public by the Gallup Poll, and have found favor with a majority of those surveyed.

If the electoral process is to function at the highest level, then each party should be represented in the election campaign by the ablest man.

In this search for able individuals who are willing to run for public office, even at great personal sacrifice, the public opinion poll can be of great help. In fact, surveys have revealed that an extraordinary number of the nation's ablest citizens, representing all fields of endeavor, would stand for any elective office, from the mayor of their city on up to the presidency.

Specifically, they would become candidates—

—if they were asked to run by a committee of responsible citizens after due investigation,

—if they did not have to raise their own campaign funds,

—if they did not have to serve for more than a limited period of time and could return to their profession or calling after their time in office,

—if they did not have to take orders from a political boss but could represent what they considered the nation's best interests.

These are reasonable conditions, and if met would suffice to bring into public office men of the highest talent. A fair estimate, based upon poll findings, is that at least half of our ablest citizens would serve in public office under these conditions.

The evidence, therefore, is clear cut. There is no

dearth of able persons to fill elective office if and when politics is elevated to the same level as other callings.

The Bandwagon Myth

Election forecasts have been made in every one of the presidential contests since the days of George Washington. Every leading newspaper historically has given major attention to elections and assigned its best political experts to cover the campaigns and to make forecasts of the outcome.

In earlier days, before the advent of the modern poll, it was the customary practice of political writers for the larger metropolitan newspapers to travel about the country, talk to the man-in-the-street, and interview party leaders and candidates. In essence, they were taking their own polls.

Today, political writers and TV commentators spend less time interviewing ordinary citizens, but they do sample the opinions of party leaders and candidates, they study and compare poll results, including those taken by the parties or candidates and by the newspapers in many states.

Working with data obtained in these many ways, they are able to reach conclusions about how each state will cast its vote. They can estimate the total electoral vote for each candidate, and it is the electoral vote that decides the winner.

On the basis of their own surveys, these writers and commentators are in a position to make a firm election prediction which, typically, they do and usually with a high measure of success.

Do such predictions influence voters?

Concern about the possible influence of election forecasts on voters developed with the advent of the "straw" polls conducted by the Literary Digest. The first of these was taken in the 1920 election, and dealt with the popularity of presidential hopefuls in the pre-convention period.

The accuracy of the Literary Digest's straw polls in the elections of 1924, 1928, and 1932 led Congressman Walter Pierce of Oregon to introduce bills in Congress to forbid the publication of poll results. He feared that such publication would create a bandwagon effect and would keep voters from participating in elections, since they would know in advance the outcome.

The question of the possible influence of poll findings on the electorate arises in every election. Because poll results are reported in figures, it is presumed that they carry more weight with voters than do the predictions of political writers and commentators. For this reason, most of the criticism about the influence of forecasts on voters has been directed at polls. Efforts to control, or to forbid, by law, the publication of poll results would necessarily have to be aimed at the reporting of results in figures instead of words—a nice legal distinction that would be difficult to make.

One of the nation's leading television commentators poses a question often put to poll takers. He asks:

"What defense do you make to suggestions that polls should be forbidden or restricted in advance of elections on the grounds that their findings unduly influence elections?"

The issue, stated in another way, is whether a forecast that a given candidate is ahead will actually lead an appreciable number of voters who wish to be on the winning side to clamber aboard his bandwagon.

It would be foolish to argue that no one is influenced by this desire to be with the winner, and yet it can be stated positively that not one single scientifically controlled study—either in the U.S. or abroad —has shown that a measureable number of people shift their votes because of poll findings in election campaigns. On the other hand, there is a mountain of evidence to show that the bandwagon theory is mostly myth.

Polls do have an influence on the conduct of government and the planning of political campaigns for the obvious reason that no better way exists to gauge the opinions and preferences of voters. But this impact of polls on political decisions has little or nothing to do with the fear entertained by many that the publication of poll results leads an appreciable number of persons to switch sides in an election campaign just to be on the winning side.

During the period since 1935 a great amount of evidence has been amassed on this point. Up to the present time (1976) political sentiment has been reported in the 20 national elections—presidential and congressional—held since 1935.

If there were a tendency for voters to climb aboard the bandwagon, the publication of poll results, showing one candidate ahead, would inevitably increase the lead of the favored candidate. Some persons who preferred or were leaning toward Candidate A, on learning that his opponent, Candidate B, was actually ahead in the polls, would switch allegiance from A to B. And, if this were the case, then the polling organization in its next survey should find that Candidate B had increased his lead. By the same line of reasoning, Candidate A would have lost some of his followers.

This situation, however, is rarely found in actual experience. More often than not, and for reasons that will be explained later, the losing candidate tends to narrow the gap as the campaign nears election day. The campaign of 1968 can be cited as an example. In that campaign, Richard Nixon started out far ahead of Hubert Humphrey; at the end they were separated by an eye-lash. In the 1964 presidential race, President Lyndon Johnson started the race even farther ahead of Senator Barry Goldwater, but Johnson did not gain ground; he lost ground all through this campaign. In 1960, there was little change; both candidates, Richard Nixon and John F. Kennedy, were almost even at the beginning of the race and ended in a virtual tie.

Probably the classic case to demonstrate that the bandwagon theory is political myth is the presidential election of 1948. In that campaign, all the polls showed Governor Thomas E. Dewey on top. Every major political writer in America forecast a victory for Dewey, and the public itself, when asked in a survey just before the election to tell which candidate they *believed* would be elected, said "Dewey." Here was an ideal occasion to test the bandwagon theory. If the public's voting had been influenced solely by the desire to be on the winning side, Dewey would have won this election by one of the greatest landslides in history.

The many facets of the problem of the influence of polls on the electorate have been studied by experts in the field of public opinion research. One of the best and most complete reviews of the studies that have been conducted on this subject is contained in a book written by Irving Crespi and Harold Mendelsohn: *Polls, Television, and the New Politics.* This book is strongly recommended to those wishing to delve into the bandwagon theory at greater length.

A specific suggestion for a controlled study comes from an editor of one of the nation's newsmagazines, who asks:

> "*Has any study ever been done, with controls, on the bandwagon effect? Has anyone ever polled two nearby towns, for example . . . to see whether poll figures prove to be self-fulfilling to some degree, as many people suspect?*"

One study, not exactly like this, but with many similarities, was conducted by the Gallup Poll in its earlier years. Cities in which a sponsoring newspaper published Gallup Poll results were matched against cities where poll results were not published in the local newspaper. In addition, as a further check, each person interviewed in both cities was asked if he knew which candidate the polls were showing in the lead. When those who knew what the polls were showing were then compared with persons in the same education and income level who did not know, the preferences of the two groups were found to be almost identical.

Another interesting point is raised by a well-known U.S. senator who observes:

> *"The bandwagon effect is, of course, a problem of political polls. But I believe sometimes the public resents being outguessed by a computer and that sometimes Americans simply vote the opposite to the polls just for spite."*

Undeniably, some individuals may resent being treated as a statistic but their resentment does not go so far as to induce them to shift their votes from one candidate to another.

This same observation applies to the "underdog" theory—the opposite of the bandwagon theory. Even though many voters may feel genuinely sorry for a candidate who is showing up poorly in poll results, this fact, in itself, has not been influential in changing votes.

A comment by a West Coast columnist has a bearing on this point.

> *"I do not think that the polls—or even TV's early listing of the votes on election day can change the mind of the average guy to make him go along with a winner. Those who voted for Goldwater in 1964 did not expect him to win, and here in California, even when the first returns marked LBJ as almost a certain winner, Goldwaterites still went to the polls to vote for their man. (I was one of them.)"*

In the presidential election of 1968 many persons who voted for George Wallace did not expect him to win. They voted for him largely to register their protest about the state of affairs and the major party candidates.

The obvious fact is that political attitudes are firmly implanted in the typical voter's value and belief system. They are a product of many factors, some reaching back into the voter's early life.

The tenacity with which political attitudes are held helps to explain why the endorsement of candidates by well known and highly respected leaders—(or by newspapers, for that matter)—carries so little weight with voters.

One of the most revealing experiences of the writer,

in this respect, goes back to the election campaign of 1940, the year when Wendell Willkie opposed Franklin D. Roosevelt. At that time, John L. Lewis was the revered head of the United Mine Workers.

Lewis gave his full support to Willkie. Believing that this strong endorsement might change the political line-up of the state of Pennsylvania, the Gallup Poll rushed a team of interviewers into the state's coal regions to measure the effect of the Lewis announcement. The result of the survey showed that the followers of John L. Lewis had budged scarcely one percentage point away from their early and overwhelming support of F.D.R. found in an earlier survey.

The expenditure of money on advertising and other types of promotion can be important to a candidate who is not well known to the electorate. But when he is well known, the money spent for this purpose has far less effect than one might expect. For example, during the hotly contested race for the G.O.P. nomination in 1968, large sums were spent on television commercials by the Rockefeller organization to gain support for its candidate among the rank and file of the party, and to win the support of independent voters in the effort to offset Nixon's strength with the local leaders of the Republican Party. But even this heavy expenditure of money brought little or no change in the recorded popular strength of Governor Rockefeller.

President Nixon, himself, learned the same lesson two years later. In the 1970 congressional campaign, the G.O.P. was well supplied with cash and could buy ample television time. The Democrats, on the other hand, were broke and had to scratch about even to get enough money to make a final plea for their candidates on the eve of the election. Even with the heavy expenditure of money, little benefit accrued to the Republican side. Poll findings showed almost exactly the same results at the end of the campaign as they did at the beginning.

Debate over the possible influence of polls on the senatorial race in New York State in the 1970 election will probably continue for years. Senator Charles Goodell, then incumbent Republican senator, opposed James Buckley, running on the Conservative Party ticket and Congressman Ottinger, the Democratic candidate.

The Daily News poll showed Goodell in third place with Buckley heading the list. This posed a problem for the many liberals who supported Goodell: should they shift from Goodell to Ottinger to forestall a victory by a right-wing conservative? Ottinger and Buckley were running a close enough race so that any sizeable shift by Goodell's liberal followers would enable Ottinger to win. Buckley won the election, as the polls had indicated.

Referring to this election, a U.S. senator asks:

"Could not the Daily News poll have been self-fulfilling in predicting a poor third showing for Goodell; did this 'stampede' many

Goodell supporters onto the Ottinger line—
supporters who would have stuck with Goodell
were it not for the News poll telling them that
Goodell did not have a chance?"

In his comments attached to a bill which Senator
Goodell introduced in the Senate in his final days in
office, to require polls to disclose their procedures, he
made this statement:

"A dismaying number of voters appeared to be
making election decisions upon the basis of
poll results whose accuracy they could not
evaluate."

Full disclosure of poll procedures has been a practice followed and recommended by the Gallup Poll
from its beginning. In 1940, in *The Pulse of
Democracy,* I wrote:

"The public is entitled to know all the facts about
polls of public opinion. The people should be informed of the nature of the sponsorship of various
polls and should know where the money for polls
comes from. They are entitled to know the method of
collecting the ballots and the margins of error within
which the published figures are to be interpreted."

In light of this, it is my opinion that Senator
Goodell made a proper request of the *Daily News* to
disclose the polling methods employed, since the results of the *Daily News* poll conflicted with his own
poll results and with those of the Harris organization,
employed by the *Daily News* to cover the same
election.

Poll results should also have been published with some explanation of the average margin of error that the *Daily News* polls had registered in previous elections.

As it turned out, the poll results reported by the *Daily News* were reasonably close to the official returns. And in this election, full disclosure of polling methods and the margin of error would not likely have changed the situation for Senator Goodell.

This senatorial race in New York does involve a principle somewhat different from that embraced in the bandwagon theory. It involves a matter of political strategy based upon poll findings.

If it is proper and legitimate for candidates and parties to use poll results to guide campaign strategy, is it not legitimate and proper for the voter, himself, to have the same privilege in deciding how to cast his vote?

To be specific, if liberal voters, by making the shift from Goodell to Ottinger, had succeeded in their effort to defeat the conservative candidate, or had the Ottinger voters switched to Goodell, they could rightfully credit the *Daily News* poll for supplying the political data to enable them to defeat the conservative candidate.

Section 2

HOW POLLS OPERATE

The Cross-Section

The most puzzling aspect of modern polls to the layman is the cross-section or sample. How, for example, is it possible to interview 1,000 or 2,000 persons out of a present electorate of about 150 million and be sure that the relatively few selected will reflect accurately the attitudes, interests, and behavior of the entire population of voting age?

One of America's most respected political writers makes this comment:

> *"I think the doubts, if any, of those in my field (political commentators) center on the validity of the sample. How do you settle upon a sample; how do you keep it up to date; what changing conditions do you consider, and whether a group that might suffice for polling a presidential election differs—if it does— from one on which you might test various issues?"*

Unless the poll watcher understands the nature of sampling and the steps that must be taken to assure its representativeness, the whole operation of scientific polling is likely to have little meaning, and even less significance, to him.

With the goal in mind of making the process understandable, and at the risk of being too elementary, I have decided to start with some simple facts about the nature of sampling—a procedure, I might add, that is as old as man himself.

When a housewife wants to taste the quality of the soup she is making, she tastes only a teaspoonful or two. She knows that if the soup is thoroughly stirred, one teaspoonful is enough to tell her whether she has the right mixture of ingredients.

In somewhat the same manner, a bacteriologist tests the quality of water in a reservoir by taking a few samples, maybe not more than a few drops from a half-dozen different points. He knows that pollutants of a chemical or bacteriological nature will disperse widely and evenly throughout a body of water. He can be certain that his tiny sample will accurately reflect the presence of harmful bacteria or other pollutants in the whole body of water.

Perhaps a more dramatic example is to be found in the blood tests given routinely in clinics and hospitals. The medical technician requires only a few drops of blood to discover abnormal conditions. He does not have to draw a quart of blood to be sure that his sample is representative.

These examples, of course, deal with the physical world. People are not as much alike as drops of water, or of blood. If they were, then the world of individuals could be sampled by selecting only a half-dozen persons anywhere. People are widely different because their experiences are widely different.

Interestingly, this in itself comes about largely through a sampling process. Every human being gathers his views about people and about life by his own sampling. And, it should be added, he almost invariably ends with a distorted picture because his experience is unique. For example, he draws conclusions about "California" by looking out of his car or airplane window, by observing the people he meets at the airport or on the streets, and by his treatment in restaurants, hotels, and other places. This individual has no hesitancy in telling his friends back home what California is really like—although his views, obviously, are based upon very limited sampling.

The black man, living his life in the ghetto, working under conditions that are often unpleasant and for wages that are likely to be less than those of the white man who lives in the suburban community, arrives at his own views about racial equality. His sample, likewise, is unrepresentative even though it may be typical of fellow blacks living under the same conditions. By the same token, well-to-do whites living in the suburbs with the advantages of a college education and travel have equally distorted views of equality. These distortions come about because their sampling, likewise, is based upon atypical experiences.

Although every individual on the face of the earth is completely unique, in the mass he does conform to certain patterns of behavior. No one has expressed this better than A. Conan Doyle, author of the Sherlock Holmes series. He has one of his characters make this observation:

"While the individual man is an insoluble puzzle, in the aggregate he becomes a mathematical certainty. You can never foretell what any one man will do, but you can say with precision what an average number will be up to. Individuals vary, but averages remain constant."

Whenever the range of differences is great—either in nature or man—the sampling process must be conducted with great care to make certain that all major variations or departures from the norm are embraced.

Since some differences that exist may be unknown to the researcher, his best procedure to be sure of representativeness is to select samples from the population by a chance or random process. Only if he follows this procedure can he be reasonably certain that he has covered all major variations that exist.

This principle can be illustrated in the following manner. Suppose that a government agency, such as the Bureau of the Census, maintained an up to date alphabetical list of the names of all persons living in the United States 18 years of age and older. Such a file, at the present time, would include approximately 148 million names.

Now suppose that a survey organization wished to draw a representative sample of this entire group, a sample, say of 10,000 persons. Such a representative sample could be selected by dividing 148,000,000 by 10,000—which produces a figure of 14,800. Now if the researcher goes systematically through the entire file and records the name of every 14,800th listed, he can be sure that his sample is representative.

The researcher will find that this chance selection, in the manner described, has produced almost the right percentage of Catholics and Protestants, the proper proportion of persons in each age and education level. The distribution of persons by occupation, sex, race, and income should be broadly representative and consistent with the best available census data. It is important, however, to emphasize the words "broadly representative." The sample—even of 10,000—most likely would not include a single person belonging to the Fox Indian Tribe or a single resident of Magnolia, Arkansas. It might not include a single citizen of Afghanistan heritage, or a single Zoroastrian.

For the purposes served by polls, a sample normally needs to be only broadly representative. A study could be designed to discover the attitudes of American Indians, in which case the Fox Indians should be properly represented. And a specially designed study of Arkansas would likely embrace interviews with residents of Magnolia.

But for all practical purposes, individuals making up these groups constitute such a small part of the whole population of the United States that their inclusion, or exclusion, makes virtually no difference in reaching conclusions about the total population or even of important segments of the population.

Unfortunately, there is no master file in the United States of persons over the age of 18 that is available to the researcher. Moreover, even a few weeks after the decennial census such a file would be out of date. Some citizens would have died, some would have moved, and still others would have reached the age of 18.

Unlike some European countries, no attempt is made in the United States to keep voter registration lists complete and up to date. Because of this failure to maintain accurate lists of citizens and of registered voters, survey organizations are forced to devise their own systems to select samples that are representative of the population to be surveyed.

Any number of sampling systems can be invented so long as one all-important goal is kept in mind. Whatever the system, the end result of its use must be to give every individual an equal opportunity of being selected.

Perhaps not every individual, since some persons will be hospitalized, some in mental or penal institutions, some in the armed forces in foreign lands. While these individuals help make up the total U.S. citizenry, most are disenfranchised by the voting laws of the various states or find difficulty in implementing their opinions at election time. Typically, therefore, they are not included in survey cross-sections.

The Gallup Poll has designed its sample by choosing at random not individuals as described previously, but small districts such as census tracts, census enumeration districts, and townships. A random selection of these small geographical areas provides a good starting point for building a national sample.

The U.S. population is first arranged by states in geographical order and then within the individual states by districts, also in geographical order. A sampling interval number is determined by dividing the total population of the nation by the number of interviewing locations deemed adequate for a general purpose sample of the population 18 years of age and older. In the case of the Gallup Poll sample, the number of locations, so selected, is approximately 300.

At the time of this writing, the population of the U.S. 18 years and older is 148,000,000. Now dividing 148,000,000 by 300 yields a sampling interval of 490,-000. A random starting number is then chosen between 1 and 490,000 in order to select the first location. The remaining 299 locations are determined by the simple process of adding 490,000 successively until all 300 locations are chosen throughout the nation.

A geographical sampling unit having been designated, the process of selection is continued by choosing at random a given number of individuals within each unit. Conceivably this might be a Census tract in Scranton, Penna. Using block statistics, published by the Census Bureau for cities of this size, a block, or a group of blocks, within the tract is chosen by a random method analogous to the procedure used to select the location.

Within a block or groups of blocks so selected, the interviewer is given a random starting point. Proceeding from this point, the interviewer meets his assignment by taking every successive occupied dwelling. Or, as an alternative procedure, he can be instructed to take every third or every fifth or every nth dwelling unit and to conduct interviews in these designated homes.

In this systematic selection plan, the choice of the dwelling is taken out of the hands of the interviewer. As a reminder to the reader, it should be pointed out that the area or district has been selected by random procedures; next, the dwelling within the district has been chosen at random. All that now remains is to select, at random, the individual to be interviewed within the household.

This can be done in several ways. A list can be compiled by the interviewer of all persons of voting age residing within each home. From such a household list, he can then select individuals to be interviewed by a random method. Ingenious methods are employed to accomplish this end. One survey organization in Europe, for example, instructs the interviewer to talk to the person in the household whose birthday falls on the nearest date.

Now the process is complete. The district has been selected at random; the dwelling unit within the district has been selected at random; and the individual within the dwelling unit has been selected at random. The end result is that every individual in the nation of voting age has had an equal chance of being selected.

This is the theory. In actual practice, problems arise, particularly in respect to the last stage of the process. The dwelling unit chosen may be vacant, the individual selected within a household may not be at home when the interviewer calls. Of course, the interviewer can return the next day; in fact, he or she can make a half-dozen call backs without finding the person. Each call back adds that much to the cost of the survey and adds, likewise, to the time required to complete the study.

Since no nationwide survey has ever reached every person designated by any random selection procedure, special measures must be employed to deal with this situation.

Even with a dozen call backs, some individuals are never found and are never interviewed. They may be in the hospital, visiting relatives, on vacation, on a business trip, not at home except at very late hours, too old or too ill to be interviewed—a few may even refuse to be interviewed.

The goal, of course, is to reach the greatest number of the originally designated persons.

To deal with this problem, the Gallup Poll introduced in the early 1950's, a system called Time-Place interviewing. After an intensive study of the time of day when different members of a household are at home, an interviewing plan was devised that enabled interviewers to reach the highest proportion of persons at the time of their first call.

Since most persons are employed outside the home, interviewing normally must be done in the late afternoon and evening hours, and on week-ends. These are the times when men, and especially younger men, are likely to be at home, and therefore available to be interviewed.

In various nations, survey organizations are working out new ways to meet this problem of the individual selected for the sample who is not at home.

These new procedures may meet more perfectly the ideal requirements of random sampling.

How does this system of sampling compare with what is known as "quota sampling?"

Many ardent advocates of the procedure described as "quota sampling" are still to be found. This, it should be pointed out, was the system generally employed by the leading survey organizations in the pre-1948 era.

The quota system is simplicity itself. If the state of New York has 10 per cent of the total population of the United States, then 10 per cent of all interviews must come from this state. In the case of a national sample of 10,000, this would mean 1,000 interviews.

Going one step farther, since New York City contains roughly 40 per cent of the population of the state, then 40 per cent of the 1,000 interviews must be allocated to New York City, or 400. And since Brooklyn has roughly a third of the total population of New York City, a third of the 400 interviews, or 133, must be made in this borough. In similar fashion, all of the 1,000 interviews made in the state of New York can be distributed among the various cities, towns, and rural areas. Other states are dealt with in similar fashion.

Making still further use of census data, the interviews to be made in each city, town, or rural areas can be assigned on an occupational basis: so many white-collar workers, so many blue-collar workers, so many farmers, so many business and professional people, so many retired persons, and so many on the welfare rolls. The allocation can also be made on the basis of rents paid. The interviewer, for example, may be given a "quota" of calls to be made in residential areas with the highest rental values, in areas with medium priced rentals, and in low rental areas. Typically, in the quota sampling system, the survey organization predetermines the number of men and women, the age, the income, the occupation, and the race of individuals assigned to each interviewer.

In setting such quotas, however, important factors may be overlooked. In 1960, for example, a quota sample that failed to assign the right proportion of Catholic voters would have miscalculated John Kennedy's political strength. An individual's religious beliefs, obviously, cannot be ascertained by his appearance or by the place where he dwells; this applies to other factors as well.

Not only do theoretical considerations fault the quota system, but also the problems that face the interviewer. When the selection of individuals is left to him, he tends to seek out the easiest-to-interview respondents. He is prone to avoid the worst slum areas, and consequently he turns up with interviews that are likely to be skewed on the high income and education side. Typically, a quick look at the results of quota sampling will reveal too many persons with a college education, too many persons with average and above average incomes, and in political polls, too many Republicans. Therefore, one of the many advantages of the random procedure is that the selection of respondents is taken out of the hands of the interviewer. In the random method, the interviewer is told exactly where to go and when to go.

A political commentator asks:

"How are cross-sections kept up-to-date?"

Samples designed in 1960 are obviously out of date by 1970—and in the case of fast growing areas, even in a year or two.

Although America's population is highly mobile, the basic structure of society changes little. Perhaps the greatest change in America in recent years has been the rising level of education. In 1935, when the Gallup Poll first published poll results, only 7.2 per cent of the adult population had attended college for one year or more. Today that figure is 27 per cent.

How does a research organization know that the sample it has designed meets proper standards? Normally, examination of the socio-economic data gathered by the interviewer at the end of each interview provides the answer. As the completed interview forms are returned from the field to the Princeton office of the Gallup Poll, the facts from each are punched into IBM cards. In addition to the questions that have dealt with issues and other matters of interest, the interviewer has asked each person to state his occupation, age, how far he went in school, his religious preference, whether he owns or rents his dwelling, and many other questions of a factual nature.

Since the Census Bureau Current Population Surveys provide data on each one of these factors, even a hasty examination will tell whether the cross-section is fairly accurate, that is, whether the important factors line up properly with the known facts, specifically:

—the educational level of those interviewed
—the age level
—the income level
—the proportion of males to females
—the distribution by occupations
—the proportion of whites to non-whites
—the geographical distribution of cases
—the city-size distribution.

Typically, when the educational level is correct, that is, when the sample has included the right proportion of those who have attended college, high school, grade school, or no school, when the geographical distribution is right and all areas of the nation have been covered in the correct proportion, when the right proportion of those in each income level has been reached, and the right percentage of whites and non-whites, of men and women—then usually other factors tend to fall in line. These include such factors as religious preference, political party preference, and most other factors that bear upon voting behavior, buying behavior, tastes, interests, and the like.

"But aren't some people not represented in a national sample?"

After checking all of the above "controls" it would be unusual to find that every group making up the total population is represented in the sample in the exact percentage that it should be. Some groups may be slightly larger or smaller than they should be. The non-white population 18 years and older, which makes up 11 per cent of the total population, may be found to be less, or more, than this percentage of the returned interviews. Those who have attended high school in the obtained interviews may number 58 per cent when actually the true figure should be 54 per cent.

Ways have been developed to correct situations such as these which arise out of the over-representation or under-representation of given groups. The sample can be balanced, that is, corrected so that each group is included in the proportion it represents in the total population. When this procedure is followed, the assumption is made that persons within each group who are interviewed are representative of the group in question. But there are obvious limitations to this. If only a few persons are found in a given category then the danger is always present that they may not be typical or representative of the people who make up this particular group or cell.

On the whole, experience has shown that this process of weighting by the computer actually does produce more accurate samples. Normally, results are changed by only negligible amounts—seldom by more than one or two percentage points.

"Is a new sample used for each new issue polled?"

A persistent misconception about polling procedures is that a new sample must be designed for measuring each major issue. Actually, Gallup Poll cross-sections are always based upon samples of the entire voting age population. Every citizen has a right to voice his opinion on every issue and to have it recorded. For this reason, all surveys of public opinion seek to reach a representative cross-section of the entire population of voting age.

"Do you go back to the same persons?"

The answer, in the case of the Gallup Poll, is "no." The same person is not interviewed again. Some survey research is based upon fixed cross-sections or "panels". The same persons are re-interviewed from time to time to measure shifts in opinion. There are certain advantages to this system—it is possible to determine to what extent over-all changes cloak individual changes. But a practical disadvantage is that the size of the sample remains fixed. Unless the panel is very large, reliable information cannot be produced for smaller subgroups. In the case of the Gallup Poll, the same question can be placed on any number of surveys and the total sample expanded accordingly, since the same persons are not re-interviewed.

Panels have other limitations. One has to do with determining the level of knowledge. Having asked a citizen what he knows about a certain issue in the first interview, he may very well take the trouble to read about it when he sees an article later in his newspaper or magazine. There is, moreover, a widespread feeling among researchers that the repeated interviewing of the same person tends to make him a "pro" and to render him atypical for this reason. But the evidence is not clear-cut on this point. The greatest weakness, perhaps, is that panels tend to fall apart; persons change their place of residence and cannot be found for a second or subsequent measurement; some refuse to participate more than once and must be replaced by substitutes.

The subject of election polling will be dealt with at length in a later section of this book. At this point, however, one of the questions posed at the beginning of this section dealing with cross-sections needs to be answered.

"Does a group that might suffice for polling a presidential election differ from one used to test various issues?"

The answer has already been given—the same sample suffices for both purposes. Always the starting point is the total voting-age population. In the case of elections, non-registered voters must be screened out, and in the final stages of the campaign, the registered voters who are not likely to vote must also be excluded.

Later the procedures for filtering out the non-registered voters, and those unlikely to vote among the registered voters, will be explained in some detail. Suffice it to say here that this is one of the most difficult and delicate research tasks in the whole polling operation and one that is most likely to prove a stumbling block to the amateur researcher.

The Size of Samples

Questions on sample size come from many sources. The publisher of one of America's leading magazines makes this comment:

"I hope that you demonstrate that if the sample is properly constructed you need poll only about 1,500 persons to get an adequate sample of the entire U.S. I still run into very intelligent people who believe that a nationwide poll is meaningless unless about 50,000 are polled."

A United States Senator says:

"How do you answer the person who says he does not know of anyone who has ever been polled?"

The Washington correspondent of a large Midwest daily comments:

"In more than 40 years of newspapering around this country, and the world for that matter, I have never met anyone who admitted to being polled by a public opinion poll and I have met a lot of people."

The likelihood of any single individual, 18 or older, being polled in a sample of 1,500 persons is about one chance in 90,000. With samples of this size, and with the frequency that surveys are scheduled by the Gallup Poll, the chance that any single individual will be interviewed—even during a period of two decades —is less than one in two hundred.

An early experience of the writer illustrates dramatically the relative unimportance of numbers in achieving accuracy in polls and the vital importance of reaching a true cross-section of the population sampled.

In the decade preceding the 1936 presidential election, the Literary Digest conducted straw polls during elections and with a fair measure of success. The Literary Digest's polling procedure consisted of mailing out millions of post card ballots to persons whose names were found in telephone directories or on lists of automobile owners.

The system worked so long as voters in average and above average income groups were as likely to vote Democratic as Republican; and conversely, those in the lower income brackets—the have-nots— were as likely to vote for either party candidate for the presidency.

With the advent of the New Deal, however, the American electorate became sharply stratified, with many persons in the above average income groups who had been Democrats shifting to the Republican banner, and those below average to the Democratic.

Obviously, a polling system that reached telephone subscribers and automobile owners—the perquisites of the better-off in this era—was certain to overestimate Republican strength in the 1936 election. And that is precisely what did happen. The Literary Digest's final pre-election poll showed Landon winning by 57% and Franklin D. Roosevelt losing with 43% of the two-party popular vote.

Landon did not win, as everyone knows. In fact, Roosevelt won by a whopping majority—62.5 per cent to Landon's 37.5 per cent. The error, more than 19 percentage points, was one of the greatest in polling history.

The outcome of the election spelled disaster for the Literary Digest's method of polling, and a boon to the new type of scientific sampling which was introduced for the first time in that presidential election by my organization, Elmo Roper's and Archibald Crossley's.

The Literary Digest had mailed out 10,000,000 post card ballots—enough to reach approximately one family in every three at that point in history. A total of 2,376,523 persons took the trouble to mark their post card ballots and return them.

Experiments with new sampling techniques had been undertaken by the writer as early as 1933. By 1935 the evidence was clear-cut that an important change had come about in the party orientation of voters—that the process of polarization had shifted higher income voters to the right, lower income voters to the left.

When the presidential campaign opened in 1936, it was apparent that the Literary Digest's polling method would produce an inaccurate figure. Tests indicated that a large majority of individuals who were telephone subscribers preferred Landon to FDR, while only 18 per cent of those persons on relief rolls favored Landon.

To warn the public of the likely failure of the Literary Digest, the writer prepared a special newspaper article which was widely printed on July 12, 1936—at the beginning of the campaign. The article stated that the Literary Digest would be wrong in its predictions and that it would probably show Landon winning with 56 per cent of the popular vote to 44 per cent for Roosevelt. The reasons why the poll would go wrong were spelled out in detail.

Outraged, the Literary Digest editor wrote: "Never before has anyone foretold what our poll was going to show even before it started . . . Our fine statistical friend (George Gallup) should be advised that the Digest would carry on with those old fashioned methods that have produced correct forecasts exactly one hundred percent of the time."

When the election had taken place, our early assessment of what the Literary Digest Poll would find proved to be almost a perfect prediction of the Digest's final results—actually within 1 percentage point. While this may seem to have been a foolhardy stunt, actually there was little risk. A sample of only 3,000 post card ballots had been mailed by my office to the same lists of persons who received the Literary Digest ballot. Because of the workings of the laws of probability, that 3,000 sample should have provided virtually the same result as the Literary Digest's 2,376,523 which, in fact, it did.

Through its own polling, based upon modern sampling procedures, the Gallup Poll, in the 1936 election, reported that the only sure states for Landon were Maine, Vermont, and New Hampshire. The final results showed Roosevelt with 56 per cent of the popular vote to 44 per cent for Landon. The error was 6.8 percentage points, the largest ever made by the Gallup Poll. But because it was on the "right" side, the public gave us full credit, actually more than we deserved.

The Literary Digest is not the only poll that has found itself to be on the "wrong" side. All polls, at one time or another, find themselves in this awkward position, including the Gallup Poll in the election of 1948. Ironically, the error in 1936—a deviation of 6.8 percentage points from the true figure—was greater than the error in 1948—5.4 percentage points. But the public's reaction was vastly different.

The failure of polls to have the winning candidate ahead in final results is seldom due to the failure of the poll to include enough persons in its sample. Other factors are likely to prove to be far more important, as will be pointed out in later pages.

"Just how do the laws of probability apply in the case of polls?"

Examination of probability tables quickly reveals why polling organizations can use relatively small samples. But first the reader should be reminded that sampling human beings can never produce findings that are *absolutely* accurate except by mere chance, or luck. The aim of the researcher is to come as close as possible to absolute accuracy.

Since money and time are always important considerations in survey operations, the goal is to arrive at sample sizes that will produce results within acceptable margins of error. Fortunately, reasonably accurate findings can be obtained with surprisingly small samples.

Again, it is essential to distinguish between theory and practice. Probability tables are based upon mathematical theory. In actual survey work, these tables provide an important guide, but they can't be applied too literally.

With this qualification in mind, the size of samples to be used in national surveys can now be described. Suppose, for example, that a sample comprises only 600 individuals. What is the theoretical margin of error? If the sample is a perfectly drawn random sample, then the chances are 95 in 100 that the results of a poll of 600 in which those interviewed divide 60% in favor, 40% opposed (or the reverse) will be within 4 percentage points of the true figure, that is, the division in the population is somewhere between 56% and 64% in favor. The odds are even that the error will be less than 2 percentage points, that is between 58% and 62% in favor, 42% to 38% opposed.

What this means, in the example cited above, is that the odds are 19 to 1 that in repeated samplings the figure for the issue would vary in the case of those favoring the issue from 56% to 64%; the percentage of those opposed would vary between 44% and 36% in repeated samples. So, on the basis of a national sample of only 600 cases, one could say that the odds are great that the addition of many cases— even millions of cases—would not likely change the majority side to the minority side.

Now, if this sample is doubled in size—from 600 to 1,200—the error factor using the 95 in 100 criterion or confidence level—is decreased from 4 percentage points to 2.8 percentage points; if it is doubled again—from 1,200 to 2,400—there is a further decrease—from 2.8 to 2.0, always assuming that the sample is a mathematically random sample.

Even if a poll were to embrace a total of 2,000,000 individuals, there would still be a chance of error, although tiny. Most survey organizations try to operate within an error range of 4 percentage points at the 95 in 100 confidence level. Accuracy greater than this is not demanded on most issues, nor in most elections, except, of course, those that are extremely close.

Obviously, in many fields an error factor as large as 4 percentage points would be completely unacceptable. In fact, in measuring the rate of unemployment, the government and the press place significance on a change as small as 0.1 per cent. At present, unemployment figures are based upon nation-wide samples carried out by the U.S. Bureau of the Census in the same general manner as polls are conducted. The government bases its findings on samples of some 50,000 persons. But samples even of this size are not sufficient to warrant placing confidence in a change as small as 0.1 per cent. And yet such a change is often headlined on the front pages as indicating a real and significant change in the employment status of the nation.

Even if one were totally unfamiliar with the laws of probability, empirical evidence would suffice to demonstrate that the amassing of thousands of cases does not change results except to a minor extent.

An experiment conducted early in the Gallup Poll's history will illustrate this point. At the time—in the middle 1930's—the National Recovery Act (N.R.A.) was a hotly debated issue. Survey results were tabulated as the ballots from all areas of the U.S. were returned. The figures below are those actually obtained as each lot of new ballots was tabulated.

NUMBER OF RETURNED BALLOTS	PER CENT VOTING IN FAVOR OF THE N.R.A.
First 500	54.9%
First 1,000	53.9
First 5,000	55.4
First 10,000	55.4
First 30,000	55.5

From these results it can be seen that if only 500 ballots had been received, the figure would have differed little from the final result. In fact the greatest difference found in the whole series is only 1.6 percentage points from the final result.

This example represents a typical experience of researchers in this field. But one precaution needs to be observed. The returns must come from a representative sample of the population being surveyed; otherwise they could be as misleading as trying to project the results of a national election from the vote registered late in the afternoon of election day in a New Hampshire village.

The theoretical error, as noted earlier, can be used only as a guide. The expected errors in most surveys are usually somewhat larger. In actual survey practice, sample design elements tend to reduce the range of error as does stratification; some tend to increase the range of error as, for example, clustering. But these are technical matters to be dealt with in textbooks on statistics.

Survey organizations should, on the basis of their intimate knowledge of their sampling procedures and the analysis of their data, draw up their own tables of suggested tolerances to enable laymen to interpret their survey findings intelligently.

"How many people does the Gallup Poll include in a typical national survey?"

The normal sampling unit of the Gallup Poll consists of 1,500 individuals of voting age, that is, 18 years and over. A sample of this size gives reasonable assurance that the margin of error for results representing the entire country will be less than 3 percentage points based on the factor of size alone.

The margin for sampling error is obviously greater for sub-groups. For example, the views of individuals who have attended college are frequently reported. Since about one-fourth of all persons over 18 years have attended college, the margin of error must be computed on the basis of one-fourth the total sample of 1,500 or 375. Instead of a margin of error of 3 percentage points, the error factor increases to 6 or 7 percentage points in the typical cluster sample.

In dealing with some issues, interest focuses on the views of subgroups such as Negroes, labor union members, Catholics, or young voters—all representing rather small segments of the total population. Significant findings for these subgroups are possible only by building up the size of the total sample.

This can be done in the case of the Gallup Poll by including the same question or questions in successive surveys. Since different, but comparable, persons are interviewed in each study, subgroup samples can be enlarged accordingly. Thus, in a single survey approximately 165 blacks and other non-whites would be interviewed in a sample of 1,500 since they constitute 11 per cent of the total voting-age population. On three successive surveys a total of 495 would be reached—enough to provide a reasonably stable base to indicate their views on important political and social issues.

Since much interest before and after elections is directed toward the way different groups in the population vote, it has been the practice of the Gallup Poll to increase the size of its samples during the final month before election day to be in a position to report the political preferences of the many groups that make up the total population—information that cannot be obtained by analyzing the actual election returns. Election results, for example, do not reveal how women voted as opposed to men, how the different age groups voted, how different religious groups voted, how different income levels voted. Many other facts about the public's voting habits can be obtained only through the survey method.

During the heat of election campaigns critics have, on occasion, asserted that the Gallup Poll increases its sample size solely to make more certain of being "right." Examination of trend figures effectively answers this criticism. The results reported on the basis of the standard sampling unit have not varied, on the average, more than one or two percentage points from the first enlarged sample in all of the national elections of the last two decades, and this, of course, is within the margin of error expected.

If a national survey can be based on as few as 1,500 persons, how many are needed to poll a city like Baton Rouge?

Persons unfamiliar with the laws of probability invariably assume that the size of the sample must bear a fixed relationship to the size of the "universe" sampled. For example, such individuals are likely to assume that if a polling organization is sampling opinions of the whole United States, a far larger sample is necessary than if the same kind of survey is to be conducted in a single state, or in a single city.

Or, to put this in another way, the assumption is that since the population of the United States is roughly ten times that of New York State, then the sample of the United States should be ten times as large.

The laws of probability, however, do not work in this fashion. Whenever the population to be surveyed is many times the size of the sample (which it typically is), the size of samples must be almost the same. If one were conducting a poll in Baton Rouge, Louisiana, on a mayoralty race, the size of the sample should be virtually the same as for the whole United States. And it goes without saying that the same principle applies to a state.

Two examples, drawn from everyday life, may help to explain this rather mystifying fact. Suppose that a hotel cook has two kinds of soup on the stove —one in a very large pot, another in a small pot. After thoroughly stirring the soup in both pots, the cook need not take a greater number of spoonsful from the large pot or fewer spoonsful from the small pot to taste the quality of the soup, since the quality should be the same.

The second example, taken from the statistician's world, may shed further light on this phenomenon. Assume that 100,000 black and white balls are placed in a large cask. The white balls number 70,000; the black balls, 30,000. Into another cask, a much smaller one, are placed 1,000 balls, divided in exactly the same proportion: 700 white balls, 300 black balls.

Now the balls in each cask are thoroughly mixed and a person, blindfolded, is asked to draw out of each cask exactly 100 balls. The likelihood of drawing 70 white balls and 30 black balls is virtually the same, despite the fact that one cask contains 100 times as many balls as the other.

If this principle were understood then hours of Senate floor time could have been saved in recent years. Senator Albert Gore, of Tennessee, a few years ago, had this to say about the Gallup Poll's sampling unit of 1,500—as reported in the Congressional Record:

> "As a layman I would question that a straw poll of less than 1 per cent of the people could under any reasonable circumstance be regarded as a fair and meaningful cross-section. This would be something more than 500 times as large a sample as Dr. Gallup takes."

In the same discussion on the Senate floor, Senator Russell Long of Lousiana added these remarks:

> "I believe one reason why the poll information could not be an accurate reflection of what the people are thinking is depicted in this example. Suppose we should try to find how many persons should be polled in a city the size of New Orleans in order to determine how an election should go. In a city that size, about 600,000 people, a number of 1,000

would be an appropriate number to sample to see how the election was likely to go. . . . In my home town of Baton Rouge, Louisiana, I might very well sample perhaps 300 or 400 people and come up with a fairly accurate guess as to how the city or the parish would go, especially if a scientific principle were used. But if I were to sample only a single person or two or three in that entire city, the chances are slim that I would come up with an accurate guess."

If the reader has followed the explanation of the workings of the laws of probability, and of earlier statements about the size of samples, he will be aware of two errors in the Senator's reasoning. Since both cities, New Orleans and Baton Rouge, have populations many times the size of the sample suggested, both require samples of the same size. The second is his assumption that any good researcher would possibly attempt to draw conclusions about either city on the basis of "a single person or two."

The size of the "universe" to be sampled is typically very great in the case of most surveys; in fact, it is usually many times the size of the samples to be obtained. A different principle applies when the "universe" is small. The size of a sample needed to assess opinions of the residents of a community of 1,000 voters is obviously different from that required for a city that is much larger. A sample of 1,000 in such a town would not be a sample, it would be, in effect, a complete canvass.

Questions About Questions

"More than anything, I suppose, the wording of your questions concerns me ... time after time I have had the impression that your questions were deliberately but subtly slanted to elicit a favorable response from the liberal point of view. Wording is crucial, and I've often wondered if your people really agonize over the wording."

The editor of a Southern newspaper and a political commentator of note posed this question. He can rest assured that the wording of every question is "agonized over."

Nothing is so difficult, nor so important, as the selection and wording of questions. In fact, most of the time and effort of the writer in his work in this field has been devoted to this aspect of polling.

The questions included in a national survey of public opinion should meet many tests: they must deal with the vital issues of the day, they must be worded in a way to get at the heart of these issues, they must be stated in language understandable to the least well educated, and finally, they must be strictly impartial in presenting the issue.

If any reader thinks this is easy, let him try to word questions on any present day issue. It is a tough and tiring mental task. And even years of experience do not make the problem less onerous.

One rule must always be followed. No question, no matter how simple, must reach the interviewing stage without first having gone through a thorough pre-testing procedure. Many tests must be applied to see that each question meets required standards.

Every survey organization has its own methods of testing the wording of questions. Here it will suffice to describe in some detail how the Gallup Poll goes about this task.

Pre-testing of questions dealing with complicated issues is carried on in the Interviewing Center maintained in Hopewell, New Jersey, by the Gallup organizations. Formerly, this Center was a motion picture theater. In the early 1950's it was converted into an interviewing center. The town of Hopewell is located in the middle of an area with a total population of 500,000—an area that includes the city of Trenton, Princeton, suburban communities, small towns, and rural districts. People, consequently, from many walks of life are available for interviewing.

Pre-testing procedures normally start with "in-depth" interviews with a dozen or more individuals invited to come to the Center. The purpose of these interviews is to find out how much thought each participant has given to the issue under consideration, the level of his or her knowledge about the issue, and the important facets that must be probed. Most of the questions asked in these sessions are "open" questions—that is, questions which ask: "What do you know about the XX problem? What do you think about it? What should the government do about it? etc. etc.

In conversations evoked by questions of this type, it is possible, in an unhurried manner, to discover how much knowledge average persons have of a given issue, the range of views regarding it, and the special aspects of the issue that need to be probed if a series of questions is to be developed.

The next step is to try out the questions, devised at this first stage, on a new group of respondents, to see if the questions are understandable and convey the meaning intended. A simple test can be employed. After reading the question, the respondent is asked to "play back" what it says to him. The answer quickly reveals whether the person being interviewed understands the language used and whether he grasps the main point of the question. This approach can also reveal, to the trained interviewer, any unsuspected biases in the wording of the question. When the language in which a question is stated is not clear to the interviewee, his typical reaction is: "Will you read that question again?" If questions have to be repeated, this is unmistakable evidence that they should be worded in a simpler and more understandable manner.

Another procedure that has proved valuable in testing questions is the self-administered interview. The respondent, without the benefit of an interviewer, writes out the answers to the questions. The advantages of this procedure are many. Answers show whether the individual has given real thought to the issue and reveal, also, the degree of his interest. If he has no opinion, he will typically leave the question blank. If he has a keen interest in the issue, he will spell out his views in some detail. And if he is misinformed, this becomes apparent in what he writes.

Self-administered questionnaires can be filled out in one's own home, or privately in an interviewing center. Since the interviewer is not at hand, many issues, such as those dealing with sex, drug addiction, alcoholism, and other personal matters can be dealt with in this manner. The interviewer's function is merely to drop off the questionnaire, and pick it up in a sealed envelope the next day—or the respondent can mail it directly to the Princeton office.

Even with all of these precautions, faulty question wordings do sometimes find their way onto the survey interviewing form. Checks for internal consistency, made when the ballots are returned and are tabulated, usually bring to light these shortcomings.

Most important, the reader, himself, must be the final judge. The Gallup Poll, from its establishment in 1935, has followed the practice of including the exact wording of questions, when this is important, in the report of the poll findings. The reader is thus in a position to decide whether the question is worded impartially and whether the interpretation of the results, based upon the question asked, is fair and objective.

———

A prominent United States senator brings up another point about questions:

"How do pollsters like yourself determine what questions to ask from time to time? It seems to me that pollsters can affect public opinion simply by asking the question. The results could be pro or anti the president depending upon the questions asked and the president's relation to it."

To be sure, a series of questions could be asked that would prove awkward to the administration, even though worded impartially, and interpreted objectively. But this would be self-defeating because it would soon become apparent to readers and commentators that the survey organization was not engaged solely in fact-finding but was trying to promote a cause.

One way to prevent unintentional biases from creeping into survey operations is to have a staff that is composed of persons representing the different shades of political belief—from right to left. If not only the questions but also the written reports dealing with the results have to run this gamut—as is the practice in the Gallup office—the dangers of unintentional bias are decreased accordingly.

Still one more safeguard in dealing with biases of any type comes about through the financial support of a poll. If sponsors represent all shades of political belief—then economic pressures alone help to keep a poll on the straight and narrow path.

So much for bias in the wording and selection of questions. This still does not answer the question posed by some who wish to know what standards or practices are followed in deciding what issues to present to the public.

Since the chief aim of a modern public opinion poll is to assess public opinion on the important issues of the day and to chart the trend of sentiment, it follows that most subjects chosen for investigation must deal with current national and international issues, and particularly those which have an immediate concern for the typical citizen. Newspapers, magazines, and the broadcast media are all useful sources of ideas for polls. Suggestions for poll subjects come from individuals and institutions—from members of Congress, editors, public officials, and foundations. Every few weeks the public itself is questioned about the most important problems facing the nation, as they see them. Their answers to this question establish priorities, and provide an up to date list of areas to explore through polling.

A widely held assumption is that questions can be twisted to get any answer you want.

In the words of one publisher:

"If you word a question one way you get a result which may differ substantially from the result you get if you word the question in a different way."

And a Senator representing a southwestern state suggests:

"It would be interesting if you could show

just how polls can be distorted to prove just about any point."

It's not that easy. Questions can be worded in a manner to bring confusing and misleading results. But the loaded question is usually self-defeating because it is obvious that is is biased.

Hundreds of experiments with a research procedure known as the split-ballot technique (one-half the cross-section gets Question A, the other half Question B) have proved that even a wide variation in question wordings did not bring substantially different results if the basic meaning or substance of the question remained the same.

Change the basic meaning of the question, add or leave out an essential part, and the results will change accordingly, as they should. Were people insensitive to words—if they were unable to distinguish between one concept and another—then the whole *raison d'être* of polling would vanish.

Often the interpreters of poll findings draw inferences which are not warranted or make assumptions that a close reading of the question does not support.

A magazine editor observes:

"It would be interesting to see the results of the same question asked two different ways."

He suggests these two wordings:

"Do you feel the United States should have gotten involved in Vietnam in the first place?"

"Do you feel the United States should have helped South Vietnam to defend itself?"

___

While at first glance these questions seem to deal with the same point, America's involvement, actually they are probing widely different aspects of involvement. In the first case, the respondent reads in "with our own troops"—in the second question, that our help will be limited to materials. Many polls have shown that the American people are willing to give military supplies to almost any nation in the world that is endangered by the Communists, but they are unwilling to send troops.

If the two questions cited above did not bring substantially different results, then all the other poll results dealing with this issue would be misleading.

Questions must be stated in words that everyone understands, and results are likely to be misleading to the extent that the words are not fully understood. Ask people whether they are disturbed about the amount of pornography in their magazines and newspapers and you will get one answer; if you talk about the amount of smut you will get another.

Word specialists may insist that every word in the language conveys a slightly different connotation to every individual. While this may be true, the world (and polls) must operate on the principle that commonly used words convey approximately the same meaning to the vast majority. And this fact can easily be established in the pre-testing of questions. When a question is read to a respondent and he is then asked to "play it back" in his own words, it becomes quickly evident whether he has understood the words, and in fact, what they mean to him.

Some questions which pass this test can still be faulty. The sophisticated poll watcher should be on the alert for the "desirable goal" question. This type of question ties together a desirable goal with a proposal for reaching this end. The respondent typically reacts to the goal as well as to the means. Here are some examples of desirable goal questions:

"To win the war quickly in Vietnam, would you favor all-out bombing of North Vietnam?"
"To reduce crime in the cities, would you favor increasing jail and prison sentences?"
"In order to improve the quality of education in the U.S., should teachers be paid higher salaries?"

These questions which present widely accepted goals accompanied by the tacit assumption that the means suggested will bring about the desired end, produce results biased on the favorable side.

The more specific questions are, the better. One of the classic arguments between newspapers and television has centered around a question that asks the public: "Where do you get most of your news about what's going on in the world today—from the newspaper, or radio, or television, or magazines, or talking to people, or where?" The answers show TV ahead of daily newspapers. But when this question is asked in a way to differentiate between international news, and local and state news, TV wins on international news, but the daily newspaper has a big lead on local news. A simple explanation is that the phrase:

"What is going on in the *world*?—is interpreted by the average citizen to mean in the far away places—not his home city.

People are extremely literal minded. A farmer in Ontario, interviewed by the Canadian Gallup Poll, was asked at the close of the interview, how long he had lived in the same house; specifically, the length of his residence there. The answer which came back: "twenty-six feet and six inches."

Whenever it is possible, the questions asked should state both sides of the issue. Realistic alternatives should be offered, or implied.

Looking back through the nearly four decades of polling, this aspect of question wording warrants the greatest criticism. There is probably little need to state the other side, or offer an alternative, in a question such as this: "Should the voting age be lowered to include those 18 years of age?" The alternative implied is to leave the situation as it is.

An excellent observation is made by a political scientist on the faculty of a New England college.

"Somehow more realism must be introduced into polls . . . People often affirm abstract principles but will not be willing to pay the price of their concrete application. For example, would you be willing to pay more for each box of soap you buy in order to reduce ground pollution—or $200 more for your next car in order to reduce air pollution, etc.?"

This type of question is similar to the desirable goal question. The public wants to clear the slums, wants better medical care, improved racial relations, better schools, better housing. The real issue is one of priorities and costs. The role of the public opinion poll in this situation is to shed light on the public's concern about each major problem, establish priorities, and then discover whether the people are willing to foot the bill.

The well-informed person is likely to think of the costs involved by legislation that proposes to deal with these social problems. But to the typical citizen there is no immediate or direct relationship between legislation and the amount he has to pay in taxes. Congress usually tries to disguise costs by failing to tie taxes or costs to large appropriations, leaving John Doe with the impression that someone else will pay the bill.

Still another type of question that is suspect has to do with good intentions. Questions of this type have meaning only when controls are used and when the results are interpreted with a full understanding of their shortcomings.

Examples of questions that fall into this category are those asking people if they "plan to go to church," "read a book," "listen to good music," "vote in the coming election," etc.

A widely syndicated commentator points out:

"In my own experience I've found you can get an honest answer to a straight, uncomplicated question . . . but ask for example (a woman in

particular) whether there shouldn't be more Shakespeare or opera on TV and radio, and they're invariably for it—although you couldn't drag them to either."

To the typical American the word "intend" or "plan" connotes many things ranging from "Do I think this is a good idea?", "Would I like to do it?", "Would it be good for me?", "Would it be good for other people?", etc. These and similar questions of a prestige nature reveal attitudes, but they are a poor guide to action.

Behavior is always the best guide. The person who attended church last Sunday is likely to go next Sunday, if he says he plans to. The citizen who voted in the last election and whose name is now on the registration books is far more likely to vote than the person who hasn't bothered to vote or to register even though he insists that he "plans" to do both.

Probably the most difficult of all questions to word is the type that offers the respondent several alternatives. Not only is it hard to find alternatives that are mutually exclusive; it is equally difficult to find a series that covers the entire range of opinions. Added to this is the problem of wording each alternative in a way that doesn't give it a special advantage. And finally, in any series of alternatives that ranges from one extreme of opinion to the other, the typical citizen has a strong inclination to choose one in the middle.

As a working principle it can be stated that the more words included in a question, either by way of explanation or in stating alternatives, the greater the possibilities that the question wording itself will influence answers.

Most of the mistakes in interpreting poll results come from failure to follow Harold Wilson's advice, quoted earlier, to:

"Scrutinize the form of the question and the detail of the answer."

The sophisticated poll watcher has still more questions to ask about the questions included in public opinion surveys.

A member of the editorial staff of a newsmagazine observes:

> *"On more than a few occasions I have found that I could not, were I asked, answer a poll with a 'yes' or 'no.' More likely my answer would be 'yes, but' or 'yes, if.' I wonder whether pollsters can't or just don't want to measure nuances of feeling?"*

Obviously it is the desire of a polling organization to produce a full and accurate account of the public's views on any given issue, nuances and all.

First, however, it should be pointed out that there are two main categories of questions serving two different purposes—one to *measure* public opinion, the other to *describe* public opinion. The first category has to do with the "referendum" type of question. Since the early years of polling, heavy emphasis has been placed upon this type of question which serves in effect as an unofficial national referendum on a given issue, actually providing the same results, within a small margin of error, that an official nation-wide referendum would if it were held at the same time and on the same issue.

At some point in the decision process, whether it be concerned with an important issue before Congress, a new law before the state legislature, or a school bond issue in Central City, the time comes for a simple "yes" or "no" vote. Fortunately, or unfortunately, there is no lever on a voting machine that permits the voter to register a "yes, if" or a "yes, but" vote. While discussion can and should proceed at length, the only way to determine majority opinion is by a simple count of noses.

If polling organizations limited themselves to the referendum type of question they would severely restrict their usefulness. They can and should use their machinery to reveal the many facets of public opinion on any issue, and to shed light on the reasons why the people hold the views which they do, in short, to explore the "why" behind public opinion.

More and more attention is being paid to this diagnostic approach and the greatest improvements in the field of public opinion research in the future are likely to deal with this aspect of polling.

One of the important developments in question technique was the development in the late 1940's of a new kind of question design that permits the investigation of views on any issue of a complex nature.

This design, developed by the Gallup Poll, has

been described as the "quintamensional approach" since it probes five aspects of opinion:

1. the respondent's awareness and general knowledge about it,
2. his over-all opinions,
3. the reasons why he holds his views,
4. his specific views on specific aspects of the problem,
5. the intensity with which he holds his opinions.

This question design quickly sorts out those who have no knowledge of a given issue. And it can even reveal the extent or level of knowledge of the interviewee about the issue.

It helps solve the problem that bothers a professor:

"Professor Converse and others have shown that on many subjects or themes there is a considerable proportion of respondents who answer without any notion of what they are really answering. How do you confront this problem?"

Since the early days of public opinion polling, the point has arisen as to the possibility of separating informed from uninformed opinion. With the quintamensional approach this is feasible—and by a very simple procedure. Few subjects are too complex or too technical to be dealt with by this question design.

This is how the system works. The first question put to the person being interviewed (on any problem or issue no matter how complex) is this: "Have you heard or read about the XXX problem (proposal or issue)?"

The person being interviewed can answer either "yes" or "no" to this question, or he can add, "I'm not sure." If he answers in the negative, experience covering many years indicates that he is being entirely truthful. If he answers "yes" or "I'm not sure" he is then asked: "Please tell me in your own words what the debate (or the proposal or issue) is about."

At this point the person interviewed must produce evidence that reveals whether he has some knowledge of the problem or issue.

The reader might imagine himself in this interviewing situation. You are called upon by an interviewer and in the course of the interview, asked if you have "heard or read about the Bronson proposal to reorganize the Security Council of the United Nations." The answer is likely to be "No." Possibly you might say: "I seem to have heard about it somewhere." Or suppose that, just to impress the interviewer (something that rarely happens) you fall into the trap of saying "yes."

The next question puts you neatly and delicately on the spot. It asks you to describe in your own words what the Bronson proposal is. You have to admit at this point that you don't know, or come up with an answer that immediately indicates you do not know what it is.

At this stage the questioning can be expanded to discover just how well informed you are. If it is an issue or proposal, then you can be asked to give the main arguments for and the main arguments against the plan or issue. In short, by adding questions at this stage, the *level* of knowledge of the respondent can be determined.

The next question in the design is an "open" question that asks simply: "What do you think should be done about this proposal?" or "How do you think this issue should be resolved?" This type of question permits the person being interviewed to give his views without any specifics being mentioned. Answers, of course, are recorded by the interviewer as nearly as possible in the exact words of the respondent.

The third category of questions seeks to find out the "why" behind the respondent's views. This can be done with a simple question asking: "Why do you feel that way?" or variations of this, along with "nondirective" probes such as: "What else?" or "Can you explain that in greater detail?", etc.

The fourth category in the design poses specific issues that can be answered in "yes" or "no" fashion. At this fourth stage it is possible to go back to those who were excluded by the first two questions: those who said they had not heard or read about the issue in question or proved, after the second question, that they were uninformed.

By explaining in neutral language to this group what the problem or issue is and the specific proposals that have been made for dealing with it, the uninformed can voice their opinions, which later can be compared with those of the already informed group.

The fifth category attempts to get at the intensity with which opinions are held. How strongly does each side hold to its views? What action is each individual willing to take to see that his opinion prevails? What chance is there that he may change his mind?

This, then, is the quintamensional approach. And its special merit is that it can quickly sort out the informed from the uninformed. The views of the well informed can be compared not only with the less well informed but with those who are learning about the issue for the first time. Moreover, through cross-tabulations, it is possible to show how special kinds of knowledge are related to certain opinions.

The filtering process may screen out nearly all individuals in the sample because they are uninformed but it is often of interest and importance to know how the few informed individuals divide on a complex issue. When the best informed individuals favor a proposal or issue, experience indicates that their view tends to be accepted by lower echelons as information and knowledge become more widespread.

But this is not the invariable pattern. In the case of Vietnam, it was the best educated and the best informed who reversed their views as the war went on. The least well educated were always more anti-Vietnam.

It is now proper to ask why, with all of its obvious

merits, this question design is not used more often. The answer is that polling organizations generally avoid technical and complex issues, preferring to deal with those on which the vast majority of Americans have knowledge and opinions. Often the design is shortened to embrace only the filter question which seeks to find out if the individual has read or heard about a given issue, and omits the other questions.

Should questions illuminate public opinion or provide the score?

In the field of public opinion research, one finds two schools of thought: one made up largely of those in academic circles who believe that research on public attitudes should be almost entirely descriptive or diagnostic; the other, made up largely of persons in political life or in journalism or allied fields, who want to know the "score."

It is the task of the polling organization to satisfy both groups. And to do this, both categories of questions must be included in the surveys conducted at regular intervals.

The long experience of the Gallup Poll points to the importance of reporting trends of opinion on all the continuing problems, the beliefs, the wishes of the people.

In fact, about four out of every ten questions included in a typical survey are for the purpose of measuring trends. Simple "yes" and "no" questions are far better suited to this purpose than "open-ended" questions, and this accounts chiefly for the high percentage of this type of question in the field of polling.

Interviewers and Interviewing Problems

Since the reliability of poll results depends so much on the integrity of interviewers, polling organizations must go to great lengths to see that interviewers follow instructions conscientiously.

A professor at an Ivy League college sums up the problems that have to do with interviewers in this question:

> *"How do you insure quality control over your interviewers, preventing them from either influencing the answers, mis-recording them, or filling in the forms themselves?"*

Before these specific points are dealt with, the reader may wish to know who the interviewers are and how they are selected and trained.

Women make the best interviewers, not only in the United States but in virtually every nation where public opinion survey organizations are established. Generally, they are more conscientious and more likely to follow instructions than men. Perhaps the nature of the work makes interviewing more appealing to them. The fact that the work is part time, is another reason why women like this type of work.

Most interviewers are women of middle age, with high school or college education. Most are married and have children; they like part-time work that takes them outside their homes.

Very few interviewers devote full time to this work. In fact, this is not recommended. Interviewing is mentally exhausting and the interviewer who works day after day at this task is likely to lose her zeal, with a consequent drop in the quality of her work.

When an area is drawn for the national cross-section—as noted in an earlier chapter—the interviewing department of the polling organization finds a suitable person to serve as the interviewer in this particular district. All the usual methods of seeking individuals who can meet the requirements are utilized, including such sources as school superintendents, newspaper editors, members of the clergy, and the classified columns of the local press.

Training for this kind of work can be accomplished by means of an instruction manual, by a supervisor, or by training sessions. The best training consists of a kind of trial-by-fire process. The interviewer is given test interviews to do after she has completed her study of the instruction manual. The trial interviews prove whether she can do the work in a satisfactory manner; more important, making these interviews enables the interviewer to discover if she really likes this kind of work. Her interviews are carefully inspected and investigated. Telephone conversations often straighten out procedures and clear up any misunderstandings about them.

Special questions added to the interviewing form

and internal checks on consistency can be used to detect dishonesty. Also, a regular program of contacting persons who have been interviewed—to see if they in fact have been interviewed—is commonly employed by the best survey organizations.

It would be foolhardy to insist that every case of dishonesty can be detected in this manner, but awareness of the existence of these many ways of checking honesty removes most if not all of the temptation for the interviewers to fill in the answers themselves.

A newsmagazine editor makes this observation:

"Although I realize that polls have built-in checks on the honesty of interviewers, I still think it's all too easy to fudge a few answers when it's late in the day and you're tired trudging through dark city streets or along a lonely rural road."

Experience of many years indicates that the temptation to "fudge" is related to the size of the work load given to the interviewer. If too many interviews are required in too short a time, the interviewer may hurry through the assignment, being less careful than she otherwise would be and, on occasion, not above the temptation to fill in a last few details.

To lessen this pressure, the assignment of interviews given to Gallup Poll interviewers has been constantly reduced through the years. At the present time, an assignment consists of only five or six interviews, and assignments come at least a week apart. This policy increases the cost per interview but it also keeps the interviewer from being subjected to too great pressure.

In the case of open questions that require the interviewer to record the exact words of the respondent, the difficulties mount. The interviewer must attempt to record the main thought of the respondent as the respondent is talking, and usually without benefit of shorthand.

The need to get something down, if only in sketchy and semi-literate manner, helps to answer in part the criticism of one newsmagazine editor who says:

> *"I come away from examining open-end questions with serious doubts about the intelligence of interviewers and their ability to handle open-end questions."*

The addition of "probe" questions to the original open-end questions helps to organize the response in a more meaningful way. In certain circumstances, the use of small tape recorders, carried by the interviewer, is highly recommended.

So much for the interviewer's side of this situation. What about the person being interviewed? How honest is he?

As one journalist asks:

> *"Is there any sure way of telling whether a per-*

son is answering truthfully, or is loading his answers for one reason or another?"

While there is no certain way of telling whether a given individual is "loading" his answers, the evidence from thousands of surveys is that people are remarkably honest and frank when asked their views in a situation that is properly structured—that is, when the respondent knows the purpose of the interview and is told that his name will not be attached to any of the things he says, and when the questions are properly worded.

It is important to point out that persons reached in a public opinion survey normally do not know the interviewer personally. For this reason, there is little or no reason to try to impress her. And, contrary to a widely held view, people are not inclined to "sound off" on subjects they know little about. In fact, many persons, entitled, on the basis of their knowledge, to hold an opinion about a given problem or issue, often hesitate to do so. In the development of the quintamensional procedure, described earlier, it was discovered that the opening question could not be stated: "Have you *followed* the discussion about the XX Issue?" Far too many said they hadn't. And for this reason the approach had to be changed to ask: "Have you *heard or read* about the XX Issue?"

The interviewer is instructed to read the question exactly as it is worded, and not try to explain it or amplify it. If the interviewee says, "Would you repeat that?" (incidentally, always the mark of a bad question) the interviewer repeats the question and if on the second reading the person does not understand or get the point of the question, the interviewer checks the "no opinion" box and goes on to the next question.

But don't people often change their minds? This is a question often asked of poll takers. The answer is, "Of course." Interviewed on Saturday, some persons may have a different opinion on Sunday. But this is another instance when the law of averages comes to the rescue. Those who shift their views in one direction will almost certainly be counterbalanced by those who change in the opposite direction. The net result is to show no change in the over-all results.

Polls can only reflect the world of people as they are—sometimes inconsistent, often uninformed. Democracy, however, does not require that every individual, every voter, be a philosopher. Democracy requires only that the sum total of individual views— the collective judgment—add up to something that makes sense.

Fortunately, there now exists some 40 years of polling evidence to prove the soundness of the collective judgment of the people.

How many persons refuse to be interviewed? The percentage is very small, seldom more than 10 per cent of all those contacted. Interestingly, this same figure is found in all the nations where public opinion polls are conducted. Refusals are chiefly a function of interviewing skill. Top interviewers are rarely turned down. This does not mean that a man who must get back to work immediately or a woman who has a cake in the oven, will take 30 to 45 minutes to discuss issues of the day. These situations are to be avoided. And that is why the Time-Place interviewing plan was developed by the Gallup Poll.

━━━━━━━━━━━━━━━━━━━━━

A Senator from a Rocky Mountain state poses this question:

> *"How do you allow for the possible embarrassment or guilty conscience factor? That is, a voter might be prepared to vote for George Wallace, but be uneasy about saying so to a stranger sitting in his living room?"*

━━━━━━━━━━━━━━━━━━━━━

When interviews and the interviewing situation are properly structured, this does not happen. The best proof of this is the example that the Senator has himself cited. In the 1968 election campaign, the Gallup Poll found Wallace, at one point, receiving as much as 19 per cent of the total vote. Later his popularity declined. The final poll result showed him with 15 per cent of the vote; he actually received 14 per cent. If there had been any embarrassment about admitting being for Wallace, his vote would obviously have been underestimated by a sizable amount.

Properly approached, people are not reluctant to discuss even personal matters—their private problems, their religion, sex. By an interesting technique developed in Sweden, even the most revealing facts about the sex life of an individual can be obtained.

And the same type of approach was found to be highly successful in finding out the extent of drug use by college students. Many studies about the religious beliefs of individuals have been conducted by the Gallup Poll without meeting interviewing difficulties.

People will talk freely if they think an important purpose is being served by giving their views and if they are assured of remaining anonymous.

The desire to have one's voice heard on issues of the day is almost universal. An interviewer called upon an elderly man and found him working in his garden. After he had offered his views on many subjects included in the poll, he called to the interviewer who had started for her car, and said: "You know, two of the most important things in my life have happened this week. First, I was asked to serve on a jury, and now I have been asked to give my views in a public opinion poll."

Measuring Intensity

To the legislator or administrator the intensity with which certain voters or groups of voters hold their opinions has special significance. If people feel strongly enough about a given issue they will likely do something about it—write letters, work for a candidate who espouses their views and against a candidate who holds a contrary view, contribute money to a campaign, try to win other voters to their candidate. To cite an example. Citizens who oppose any kind of gun control laws, though constituting a minority of the public, feel so strongly about this issue that they will do anything they can to defeat such legislation. As a result, they have succeeded in keeping strict gun laws from being adopted in most states and by the Federal government.

Since most legislation calls for more money, a practical measure of the intensity of feeling about a given piece of legislation is the willingness to have taxes increased to meet the costs.

A senator from a Midwestern state makes this criticism of polling efforts:

"Issue polling often fails to differentiate between hard and soft opinion. If the issue is national health insurance, then the real test is not whether the individual favors it but how

much more per year he is willing to pay in taxes for such a program."

This is a merited criticism of polls and, as stated earlier, one that points to the need for greater attention on the part of polling organizations. The action that an individual is willing to take—the sacrifice he is willing to undergo—to see that his side of an issue prevails, is one of the best ways of sorting out hard from soft opinion.

Questions put to respondents about "how strongly" they feel, "how important it is to them," "how much they care," etc. all yield added insights into the intensity of opinions held by the public. The fact, however, that they are used as seldom as they are in the regular polls, here and abroad, indicates that the added information gained does not compensate for the time and the difficulties encountered by the survey interviewer. Most attitude scales are, in fact, better suited to the classroom with students as captive subjects than to the face-to-face interviews undertaken by most survey organizations.

The best hope, in the writer's opinion, lies in the development of new questions that are behavior or action oriented. Here then, is an important area where both academicians and practitioners can work together in the improvement of present research procedures.

The specific complaint of the senator—that of providing a more realistic presentation of an issue—can probably be dealt with best in the question wording, as noted earlier.

While verbal scales to measure intensity can be usefully employed in many situations, two non-verbal scales have gained wide acceptance and use throughout the world. Since they do not depend upon words, language is no barrier to their use in any nation. Moreover, they can be employed in normal interviewing situations, and on a host of problems.

The scales were devised by Jan Stapel of the Netherlands Institute of Public Opinion and by Hadley Cantril and a colleague, F. P. Kilpatrick. While the scales seem to be similar, each has its own special merits.

The Stapel scale consists of a column of ten boxes. The five at the top are white, the five at the bottom black.

The boxes are numbered from +5 to −5. The interviewer carries a reproduction of this scale and at the appropriate time in the interview hands it to the respondent. The interviewer explains the scale in these, or in similar words: "You will notice that the boxes on this card go from the highest position of plus 5—something you like very much—all the way down to the lowest position of minus 5—or something you dislike very much. Now, how far up the scale, or how far down the scale would you rate the following?"

After this explanation, the interviewer asks the respondent how far up or down the scale he would rate —an individual, political party, product, company, proposal, or almost anything at issue. The person is told "put your finger on the box" which best represents his point of view; or, in other situations, to call off the number opposite the box. The interviewer duly records this number on his interviewing form.

One of the merits of the Stapel Scalometer is that it permits the person being interviewed to answer two questions with one response: whether he has a positive or a negative feeling toward the person or party or institution being rated, and at the same time the degree of his liking or disliking.

By simply calling off a number he indicates that he has a favorable or unfavorable opinion of the F.B.I., of Hubert Humphrey, of the Ku Klux Klan, and how much he likes or dislikes each. In actual use, researchers have found the extreme positions on the scale are most indicative and most sensitive to change. These are the plus 4 and plus 5 positions on the favorable side and the minus 4 and minus 5 positions on the negative side. Normally these two positions are combined to provide a "highly favorable" or a "highly unfavorable" rating.

Scale ratings thus obtained are remarkably consistent and remarkably reliable in ranking candidates and parties. In fact, the ratings given to the two major party candidates have paralleled the relative standings of the candidates in elections, especially when the party ratings are averaged with the candidate ratings.

Cantril and Kilpatrick devised the "Self-Anchoring Scale."[1] Cantril and his associate, Lloyd Free, used this scale to measure the aspirations and fears of people in different nations of the world—both those living in highly advanced countries and those in the least developed. They sought "to get an overall picture of the reality worlds in which people lived, a picture expressed by individuals in their own terms and to do this in such a way . . . as to enable meaningful comparisons to be made between different individuals, groups of individuals, and societies."

The Self-Anchoring scale is so simple that it can be used with illiterates and with people without any kind of formal education. A multi-nation survey in which this measuring instrument was employed included nations as diverse in their educational and living standards as Nigeria, India, the United States,

---

[1]F. P. Kilpatrick and Hadley Cantril. "Self-Anchoring Scale." Journal of Individual Psychology. November 1960.

West Germany, Cuba, Israel, Japan, Poland, Panama, Yugoslavia, Philippines, Brazil, and the Dominican Republic.

The scale makes use of a ladder device.

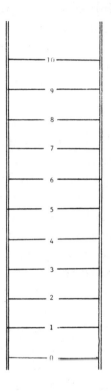

As employed in these different nations, the person being interviewed describes his wishes and hopes, as he personally sees them, and the realization of which would constitute the best possible life. This is the top anchoring point of the scale. At the other extreme, the same individual describes his worries and fears embodied in the worst possible life he can imagine. With the use of this device, he is asked where he thinks he stands on the ladder today. Then he is asked where he thinks he stood in the past, and where he thinks he will stand in the future.

This same procedure was used by Albert Cantril and Charles Roll in a survey called *Hopes and Fears of the American People*—a revealing study of the mood of the American people in the spring of 1971.

Use of this scale would be extremely useful in pursuing the goal set forth by Alvin Toffler in his book *Future Shock*. He says:

"The time has come for a dramatic reassessment of the directions of change, a reassessment made not by the politicians or the sociologists or the clergy or the elitist revolutionaries, not by technicians or college presidents, but by the people themselves. We need, quite literally, to 'go to the people' with a question that is almost never asked of them: *'What kind of a world do you want 10, 20, or 30 years from now?'* We need to initiate, in short, a continuing plebiscite on the future."

Toffler points out that:

". . . the voter may be polled about specific issues, but not about the general shape of the preferable future."

This is true to a great extent. With the exception of the Cantril-Free studies, this area has been largely overlooked by polling organizations. Toffler advocates a continuing plebiscite in which millions of persons would participate. From a practical point of view, however, sampling offers the best opportunity to discover just what the public's ideas of the future are—and more particularly, the kind of world they want 10 years, 20 years, or 30 years from now.

Reporting and Interpreting
Poll Findings

Public opinion polls throughout the world have been sponsored by the media of communication— newspapers, magazines, television and radio. It is quite proper, therefore, to answer this question asked by the editor of a newsmagazine:

"How well do the various media report and evaluate the results of a given poll?"

Since October, 1935, Gallup Poll reports have appeared weekly in American newspapers in virtually all of the major cities. During this period, I am happy to report, no newspaper has changed the wording of poll releases sent to them to make the findings fit the newspaper's editorial or political views. Editors, however, are permitted to write their own headlines because of their own special type and format policies; they can shorten articles or, in fact, omit them if news columns are filled by other and more pressing material.

Since the funds for the Gallup Poll come from this source and since the sponsoring newspapers represent all shades of political belief, the need for strict objectivity in the writing and interpretation of poll results becomes an economic as well as a scientific necessity.

At various stages in the history of the Gallup Poll, charges have been made that the poll has a Republican bias, and at other times, a Democratic bias, largely dependent upon whether the political tide is swinging towards one side or the other. Even a cursory examination of the findings dealing with issues of the day, and of election survey results, will disprove this.

The Gallup Poll is a fact-finding organization, or looked at in another way, a kind of score-keeper in the political world.

When poll findings are not to the liking of critics there is always a great temptation to try to discredit the poll by claiming that it is "biased," that it makes "secret adjustments" and that it manipulates the figures to suit its fancy, and that it is interfering with "democratic dialogue." Such charges were heard often in earlier years, but time has largely stilled this kind of attack on the poll's integrity.

Limitations of space, in the case of newspapers, and of time in the case of television and radio, impose restrictions on the amount of detail and analysis that can be included in any one report. The news media have a strong preference for "hard" news, the kind that reports the most recent score on candidate or party strength, or the division of opinion on highly controversial subjects. This type of news, it should be added, makes up the bulk of their news budgets.

These space and time requirements do require a

different kind of poll report form from one that would be written to satisfy those who prefer a full and detailed description of public opinion.

_____

A noted research and public opinion analyst associated with a Midwestern university makes this comment:

>*"Although the techniques of opinion surveying have improved greatly over the last 20 years there remains one aspect of newspaper polls which disturbs me. The abbreviated format which has become customary in the newspaper reports virtually guarantees an inadequate report of the subtleties and nuances which frequently characterize public attitudes."*

_____

The abbreviated format does limit the writer of poll reports to a few outstanding facts that emerge from the findings. Ideally, there should be a way to provide a fuller description of the subtleties and the nuances of public attitudes, a function probably best performed by scholars and academicians interested in public opinion.

As one way to stimulate this kind of analysis, the Gallup Opinion Index, published monthly, makes available all statistical data on reports issued to the press during that month. This monthly publication goes to nearly every major college and university in the U.S. and is intended primarily for students and scholars who wish additional statistical data on poll findings.

✿   ✿   ✿   ✿

Polling organizations that are members of the National Council on Published Polls have agreed that every survey report should contain the following information:

1. the public or universe sampled,
2. the method of contacting individuals comprising the sample,
3. the size of the sample,
4. the exact question or questions asked,
5. the time of interviewing, when this is important, and
6. the sponsor or sponsors of the poll when this is not obvious.

When the above facts are included in every report, the reader is in a position to reach his own conclusions. Political writers and commentators are obviously free to place their own construction on poll findings.

This answers, in part, a question posed by a nationally known and respected political writer who asks:

"To what extent are commentators either obliged or wise to accept your interpretation of your own data? What dangers do you see in one reading a poll for himself and drawing conclusions that are not necessarily yours?

This, of course, goes to the basic question of how much raw figures may be subject to various interpretations?"

A knowledgeable magazine publisher has this to say:

"I have great confidence in present-day polling techniques but I sometimes quarrel with the interpretation put on the figures. The research may be perfectly accurate, but the interpretation of it may be faulty."

One of the oddities of this new field of journalism which seeks to report "what people think," just as other branches report "what people do" is that so few political commentators have seen fit to make full use of poll data in their interpretation of the political scene.

The poll-director has a great mass of poll data. On the other hand, the political writer has a lot of insights into politics and government that the poll director does not have. Ideally, the two should work together.

❊   ❊   ❊   ❊

Poll findings are always based upon samples. The question, therefore, arises as to whether results should always be reported with the margin of error.

A political writer for a large metropolitan newspaper raises this point:

"Is it not more accurate to report a point spread instead of a simple single figure ... If so, would it not be more responsible to state it that way, even though it would take away some of the sharpness in published reports?"

Another writer makes a similar point:

"In view of the fact that there's a 2 or 3 percentage margin of error in most national sample polls, why not round off the results to the nearest multiple of 5, rather than suggest a precision that does not exist."

A degree of error is inherent in all sampling and it is important that this fact be understood by those who follow poll findings. The question is how best to achieve this end. One way, of course, is to educate the public to look at all survey results not as fixed realities or absolutes but as reliable estimates only.

An understanding of the basic facts about the laws of probability and the sampling procedure is so important today that a good case can be made for including instruction on this subject in every high school course in mathematics.

Another way to deal with the problem of sampling error is to follow the suggestion of the journalists quoted above. This concerns not only polls; it is even more important in dealing with the great and growing mass of data based upon sampling procedures now being collected and distributed by the government.

The best examples, as noted earlier, are the monthly figures on unemployment and the cost of living. Should these be published showing a point spread or the margin of error? If they were, then the monthly index of unemployment, based as it is on a sample of 50,000 would read, at a given point in time, not 8.8 per cent, but 8.5 per cent to 9.1 per cent. Reporting the cost of living index in such fashion would almost certainly cause trouble since many labor contracts are based upon changes as small as 0.1 per cent.

In reporting the trend of opinion, especially on issues, the inclusion of a point spread would make poll reports rather meaningless, particularly if the trend were not a sharp one. The character of the trend curve itself normally offers evidence of the variations due to sample size.

In the case of elections, the reporting of the margin of error can, on occasion, be misleading to the reader.

The reason is that polling errors come from many sources, as pointed out in an earlier chapter, and often the least of these in importance is the size of the sample. Yet, the statistical margin of error relates solely to this one factor.

An example may help to shed light on this point. A telephone poll taken in a mayoralty race in a large Eastern city, reported the standings of the candidates and added that they were accurate within "a possible error margin of 3.8%." In short, the newspaper in which the results were published and the polling organization assured readers that the results perforce had to be right within this margin, based upon the laws of probability. Actually, the poll figure was 14 percentage points short on the winning candidate. Factors other than the size of the sample were responsible for this wide deviation.

The best guide to a poll's accuracy is its record. If allowance is to be made for variation in the poll's reported figures, then perhaps the best suggestion, to be reasonably certain that the error will not exceed a stated amount in a national election, is to multiply by 2.5 the average deviation of the poll in its last three or four elections.

Still another way to remind readers and viewers of the presence of some degree of error in all survey findings is to find a word or words that convey this fact. A growing practice among statisticians in dealing with sampling data is to refer to results as "estimates." Unfortunately, this word conveys to some the impression that subjective judgments have entered into the process. A better word needs to be found that removes some of the certainty that is too often attached to poll percentages without, at the same time, erring in the opposite direction. The word "assessment" has been adopted by some survey researchers and it is hoped that it will come into general use in the future.

Section 3

ELECTION POLLS

Election Forecasts—Yes or No?

Public opinion research, from the beginning, has been closely identified in the public's mind with election forecasting. This is unfortunate because the prediction of election results is the least socially useful function that polls perform. Moreover, this aspect of polling stirs the greatest criticism.

The still unresolved problem is whether public opinion polls should give up election forecasting and concentrate, as a senator suggests, on:

"... *offering insights on candidates and issues.*"

In short, polls should devote time and effort to diagnosis, not prognosis.

An official of a broadcasting network makes the point in these words:

"*Just what good does it do to tell the public 24 hours in advance how they are going to vote on election day? This may make big news for the newspapers and TV but does it make any sense?*"

While the usefulness of election surveys in the future is a proper subject for debate, there can be little doubt that such reports in the past have served a valuable purpose.

It was the demonstrated accuracy of election polls, based upon scientific sampling procedures, that convinced the public and office holders that public opinion on social, political, and economic issues of the day could be gauged.

And it was the demonstrated accuracy of election polls that speeded the acceptance and use of sampling procedures in many other fields, particularly in the social sciences.

Walter Lippmann, in a prophetic statement, wrote:

> "The social scientist will acquire his dignity and his strength when he has worked out his method. He will do that by turning into opportunity the need of the Great Society for instruments of analysis by which an invisible and most stupendously difficult environment can be made intelligible."

The environment has not become less complex in the fifty years since Lippmann wrote these words. And the modern poll is at least one instrument of analysis which can and does help to make the environment more intelligible. The survey approach to social problems is widely accepted, widely employed. A leading social scientist, Kenneth Boulding, comments on the survey method in these words:

> "Perhaps the most important single development pointing towards more scientific images

of social systems is the improvement in the collection and processing of social information. The method of sample surveys is the telescope of the social sciences. It enables us to scan the social universe, at some small cost in statistical error, in ways we have never been able to do before."

The survey method has been equally important to business management. Today most of the decisions about consumer habits and needs are based upon survey findings. And it was the accuracy of election polls during recent decades that helped gain acceptance for the methods and procedures that are employed in this field of research.

The greatest value of election forecasts in the past, undoubtedly, is to be found in the improvement of such research techniques. Election results offer a criterion that permits the researcher to test the accuracy of his procedures down to the last decimal point. Except in the physical sciences, a criterion of this character is not available; researchers dealing with social or economic problems seldom know to what extent they are "on target" and because this is true they must rely heavily on secondary evidence to establish the validity of their findings.

The pressure in election polling to be "right" is great; in fact, almost overwhelming. The researcher stands naked before the whole world the day after the election. Everyone knows how far off the mark the forecast has been. No one but the poll taker risks his reputation to the same degree. And for this reason, he would be stupid not to exert every possible effort to try to improve his methods.

The question now to be asked is whether a point has been reached when the disadvantages in making election predictions outweigh the advantages.

Before examining the pros and cons of this question, one point should be clarified. Final survey figures are not, in a literal sense, forecasts or predictions. Since events, last minute statements, and shifts in campaign strategy can have an important impact upon opinion in the final days or hours before the election, the fact finder in this field has no right to turn clairvoyant and "predict" what is going to happen in the interval between the last survey and the time voters cast their ballots in the voting booth.

Unfortunately, the English language does not provide a proper word to describe this situation. Final survey figures, or "reports," are always and inevitably labelled "predictions."

I am indebted to a well-known newspaper columnist for this description of a poll:

> "Many newspaper men and other professionals I talk with don't appear to know what a poll reflects, namely what a representative cross-section of people say they think at the time they are polled—one frame in a motion picture of public opinion. If this is the correct definition of a poll, I think it needs a greater understanding among the pros."

If more people did understand that a poll is a snapshot of opinion, they would not fall into the error of assuming that every survey finding is a "prediction" of the outcome of an election that may be days, weeks, or months away.

And it answers the question posed by a newspaper publisher who comments:

"My personal opinion is that weekly polls are rather meaningless since public opinion can change so rapidly. In other words, the candidate who is leading today might find himself in a completely different position some weeks hence. This applies to other great issues as well."

Public opinion obviously does change as people learn more about candidates and their views and as they become better informed about issues. In fact, one of the most important functions that a poll can perform is to report the direction and speed of change in the public's attitudes. And trends can be determined by taking frequent measurements.

✿   ✿   ✿

Each new election in every nation, including the United States, involves new factors. It is only after the election—after the fact—that the researcher is in a position to discover the presence or absence of new factors, and to learn whether techniques he has already developed are adequate to cope with them. Something new is learned in every election, particularly if the polling organization conducts a careful post-mortem examination.

Some factors, however, can never be weighed scientifically. If corruption is widespread in a city or state and ballots are fraudulently counted, no poll technique, no matter how scientific, can take accurate account of this. The effectiveness of a political machine in getting people to the polls—even those who have no interest whatsoever in the outcome of the election—is still another factor that cannot be weighed scientifically.

Nevertheless, in the face of all of these factors, and the many others that will be described later, it is noteworthy that polls have reached a level of accuracy that will be difficult to better during the years ahead. For example, in the last 11 national elections in the United States, the average deviation of the Gallup Poll from absolute accuracy has been 1.2 percentage points. And in the last 4 elections, the deviation has been 0.8 percentage points. Unless, as some wag has observed, the laws of probability can be repealed, greater accuracy in election forecasting is not likely in the immediate future.

This should not be taken to mean that in a given election a poll won't go wrong and miss the mark by a fairly large margin. That is virtually a certainty because of the same laws of probability.

Whether to make election forecasts or not to make them is not an academic issue. At least two or three nations have seriously considered placing a legal ban on election forecasts by polls within a given number of days of the election; and in one nation the research organizations have agreed among themselves not to make election predictions. These efforts on the part of governing bodies are based upon wrong assumptions, and good sense has kept them from becoming laws. At the same time, a strong case can be made for voluntary action on the part of polling organizations to give up this part of their work, chiefly on the grounds that higher levels of accuracy are not likely to be attained, and that while refinements in techniques are always possible, no major changes are indicated at this time. And some persons still think, wrongly to be sure, that forecasts made in the final days of a campaign do interfere in a harmful way with the election process. Perhaps the most compelling reason to abandon this part of polling is that there are other and more important functions to be performed, and these merit more attention than they have been given in the past by survey organizations.

☼   ☼   ☼

Many of the ways that polls can improve the electoral process have been discussed in earlier pages. A few that relate more particularly to elections can be summarized here.

Elections do not represent the views of *all* the people. In the United States an amazingly large number of persons fail to vote. In the off-year elections fewer than half of all citizens of voting age take the trouble to cast their ballots. Even in presidential elections a third of all citizens do not bother to vote. Oddly enough, more persons fail to vote in the United States than in any other major democracy.

Polls can and do represent *all* of the people—both those who vote and those who do not vote. Findings can be reported by each group not only on candidates but on issues. Light can be shed on the reasons why people do not vote, and the measures that must be taken to induce more citizens to participate in elections.

About three in every ten persons of voting age do not align themselves with either of the two major parties, and prefer to identify themselves as "Independents." This group has no official or unofficial spokesmen, no representatives in Congress, holds no primaries or conventions, has no way to make their voices heard except through the medium of the public opinion poll.

Independent voters pose a problem to both major parties and yet the existence of this group, which is made up of individuals who switch from one major party to the other depending upon the candidates and the issues, undoubtedly works to improve the quality of candidates and government. Their views and their candidate preferences are important to both parties. They represent a force that machine politicians must take into account.

Neither of the two major parties has yet devised a system to elicit the views of their own rank and file members. In fact, there is almost no two-way communication between the party leadership and the party membership. In Great Britain and in other countries local conferences are held in which ordinary citizens can express their opinions with the certain knowledge that these views will be passed on to the leadership. In the United States, no systematic effort is made to find out the opinions of party members on issues, and only a crude and inefficient election system permits them to express their views on candidates.

Public opinion polls regularly report the views of rank and file members of both major parties on issues and candidates. In fact, in almost every Gallup Poll report will be found a statistical breakdown of survey findings for Republicans, Democrats, and Independents. Actually, the only reliable estimates of the number of persons who align themselves with the major parties are based upon poll results.

The public opinion referendum introduced by the Gallup Poll in the 1970 campaign offers the public, through the sampling process, an opportunity to express its views on all the issues that have been widely discussed during a campaign. This new procedure permits the public and elected officials to separate the popularity of candidates from the popularity of issues. And it overcomes the great weakness of trying to read "mandates" from election results.

Since official election results are the chief source of guidance for legislative programs, it is a matter of first importance that these results be properly interpreted. Unfortunately, totals only are reported by election judges. It is impossible to discover from reading official election returns how young people voted, how persons on welfare cast their ballots, how women voted, which candidates Catholics or Protestants preferred, how conservatives or liberals registered their views on candidates, how the "peace" and "war" groups voted. In some instances, it is possible to relate the vote of groups to residential areas, e.g., the poor areas of a given city cast a higher vote for Candidate A than Candidate B, but this is a crude and inexact way to determine how groups cast their votes. Only the public opinion poll can perform this function with accuracy.

Obviously the chief purpose of election campaigns is to provide ordinary citizens with the kind of information they require to make an informed, and hopefully, intelligent choice among the competing candidates. Voters need to hear issues important to the nation and important to themselves discussed and debated at length.

Present day campaigns are a mockery. Customs and practices are followed that long since have lost all meaning. The spectacle of presidential candidates running up and down streets, shaking hands with people in supermarkets, discussing trivialities, shouting old slogans and shibboleths, is not one calculated to inspire confidence either in candidates or in the democratic process. Millions of dollars are largely wasted on banners, bumper stickers, buttons, and the like.

Polls can enlighten campaign directors and candidates, showing them how to reach the people in the most effective and least expensive way; most important, polls can reveal the issues that the people want discussed, and can shed light on the reasons that are guiding their choices of candidates and parties.

In brief, polls can supply the facts needed to give elections greater meaning, they can improve the moral tone of campaigns, they can point to the reasons why so many people fail to vote, and they can make the whole electoral process more meaningful and more intelligible to the average citizen.

Election Polls
The Chief Factors
to Take Into Account

There are many kinds of polls and polling methods —some demonstrably good, some demonstrably bad. The unsophisticated make no distinction, and as Elmo Roper once pointed out, they assume simply that "a poll is a poll." When some election polls fall wide of the mark on election day the immediate— and usually gleeful—cry is heard: "The polls were wrong again." On these occasions the critics usually dump all polls into the same bag, both those that performed well and those that were far off the target. After an election, the achievements of the different polling organizations are soon forgotten and few recall the performance of any of them, except in those years such as 1948 in the United States and 1970 in Great Britain when all the major polls went astray.

As will be pointed out here and elsewhere in this book, the best and, in fact, the only way to judge a poll and the methods it employs is to look at the poll's record of accuracy achieved in the last half-dozen elections, not just in the last one. Yet, few political commentators have bothered to study these records. The unfortunate aspect of this is that polls with poor records continue to operate, usually without bothering to improve their procedures. Often, they can point to at least one election when they were "right" and that suffices to give them credence. Meanwhile, their errors are forgotten.

Again it should be emphasized that the only true measure of a poll's accuracy is not whether it happened to forecast the election of the winner, but how far its final figure—the one arrived at during the final days of a campaign—deviated from the actual division of the popular vote among the candidates or parties. This is the only scientific way to judge polling accuracy.

The critics of election polls are not entirely to blame for their failure to make proper distinction between polls and polling methods. Polling organizations have neglected to enlighten the public about their methods.

As a Governor of an Eastern state asks:

"Why are pollsters not more informative about the methods they use?"

It is assumed that every polling organization has certain "trade secrets" which it will not divulge. A national committeeman takes for granted the policy of playing things close to the chest. He comments:

"Since pollsters never give away their trade secrets, one always questions the credibility of the result."

Speaking for one organization, I can say that we have no trade secrets and never have had. Every method used by the Gallup Poll has been described in technical articles in magazines such as the *Public Opinion Quarterly*, and in books and magazine articles. But these publications, to be sure, have reached only a tiny fraction of the public—and not even very many of those persons who are immediately concerned with interpreting poll results.

Polling experience in many nations indicates that at least five major areas must be dealt with in a satisfactory manner if election surveys are to achieve a high level of accuracy.

A discussion of these factors will answer the question posed by a news commentator for a national television network:

> "What are the most important obstacles to accuracy in polling? And how can they be lessened?"

Also, a review of the present status of research in these areas will answer, in part, a political science professor who is a recognized expert in the field of election statistics. His question:

> "What improvements have been achieved in the past 40 years? Every science progresses in conceptualism, knowledge, understanding,

and technology? Has polling? And in what ways?"

Improvements in conceptualization, knowledge, and understanding have been dealt with elsewhere. Here the improvements in technology and particularly in the methods used in election polling can be detailed. As noted earlier, valuable experience has been gained from each of the 20 national elections up to this time (1976) and from the experience of affiliates and organizations in other nations where election forecasts are made.

It should be emphasized that no two polling organizations follow exactly the same procedures. Some use methods which they have developed out of their unique experience. The wide variety of procedures will answer those who raise the question:

"If polls are scientific, why don't they produce the same results?"

Surgeons in a half-dozen different hospitals who perform the same operation will each proceed in a different, but systematic manner, and with varying results. And in medicine, as in polling, it is the "success rate" that counts.

✧   ✧   ✧

The first problem in election polling is the sample. Since this subject has been dealt with at length in an earlier chapter, only one or two observations are needed here. The Gallup Poll election survey sample is based upon a random selection of election districts. In the case of election polls it is important to apply a further test—a test to see if the random selection has produced in each region of the nation a sample of districts whose voting record in the aggregate parallels that for the region. Since party allegiance is the most important single factor in determining how an individual votes, it is important to see that the sample is correct in this respect.

Other types of polls—particularly those taken by mail or by telephone—typically fail to reach, and to obtain responses from—a true cross section of the electorate. The other shortcomings of these methods will be dealt with in a following chapter.

The number of persons who must be interviewed— the size of samples needed to obtain reliable results—has also been treated elsewhere. Suffice it to say here that very few national polls have gone "wrong" because of sample size. Other factors account for their failure.

✻   ✻   ✻

The second problem in election polling involves a research task of major proportions and one that requires the most sophisticated research procedures. This is the task of sorting out those who will vote from those who will not. This is particularly a problem in the United States where so many citizens fail to vote. In the seven off-year elections since and including 1950, the percentage of the population of voting age who did not vote for candidates for the

House of Representatives has averaged 58 per cent. In the six presidential elections covering the same period, 40 per cent of all persons of voting age did not cast their ballots for presidential candidates.

If the non-voters were divided in their political preferences in the same proportion as voters, there would be no special problem. But this is not the case. In 12 elections the non-voters have been found to be appreciably more Democratic in their voting preferences—an average of 8 percentage points—to be exact. Persons least likely to vote are young adults, the very poor, Negroes, the poorly educated—groups with a higher preference for Democratic than for Republican candidates.

Paul Perry, chief architect of Gallup Poll methods and procedures, developed, as early as 1950, a scale designed to rank respondents in terms of their likelihood of voting. Since then a series of questions has been developed based on new evidence accumulated from validation studies made after each election when official voting records are examined to see if pre-election questions actually did sort out those who voted from those who did not vote.

Typically, respondents are asked if their names are on the registration books of the district where they presently reside, and if so, if they voted in the last election. This will screen out nearly 30 per cent of all voters in the weeks or months before the time is reached at the end of an election when more sophisticated procedures can be applied.

The screening process applied throughout the campaign—both in the early and late stages—produces a more accurate and more realistic appraisal of candidate strength. And it is this procedure that largely accounts for the larger G.O.P. lead reported by the Gallup Poll in the 1968 presidential campaign, than that reported by the Harris Poll. Until virtually all citizens of the United States vote, the screening process will, in most elections, screen out more Democrats than Republicans, since a higher proportion of low-income groups do not cast their ballots on election day.

      ✿   ✿   ✿

The third problem has to do with the "undecided" vote. The size of this group, depending upon the procedures used in polling, can vary from 3 or 4 per cent up to 50 per cent. Generally a high "undecided" vote is a result of bad polling techniques and poor interviewing. Normally, polls taken by telephone produce high "undecided" or "no opinion" responses.

The question of voting preference must be posed in the proper manner. In the case of the Gallup Poll, persons interviewed are always asked how they would vote if the election were being held today. They are not asked how they think they will vote one month hence or two months hence or six months hence—on election day. Many honestly do not know. It depends, in their case, on what the candidates say, the conduct of the campaign, the trend of events, and many other factors.

Most persons can answer, however, *how they feel about the candidates today,* and especially if an additional "probe" question is asked: "As of today do you lean more to Candidate X or to Candidate Y?" By asking this same question, month after month, it is possible to measure trends that occur during the weeks and months preceding election day.

❀   ❀   ❀

The fourth problem has to do with prestige.

This factor operates in many ways. Sometimes it is a negative, other times a positive factor.

———————————————————

In every election, some political commentators make statements such as these:

> *"Many voters will not admit to a pollster that they are going to vote for Wallace."*
> *"People wish others to think they are successful and that fits the Republican stereotype. So they tell interviewers that they are going to vote for the Republican candidate."*
> *"No member of a union is going to let anyone know that he plans to vote against the candidate endorsed by the union."*
> *"President X has a lot of charisma and a lot of people are going to say they plan to vote for his re-election when this is not the case."*

———————————————————

During the war years it was often said that no one would admit to an interviewer that he was going to vote against President Roosevelt, the commander-in-chief and a popular president. But these and similar comments are based upon false assumptions.

It is important to check on prestige factors such as these in every election. Even if they make a difference of one or two percentage points they would merit careful consideration on the part of the polling organization.

To check on the presence or absence of prestige factors and the extent to which they may be operating in a given election, a secret ballot technique has been evolved out of pioneering work on this problem by Sidney Goldish, first director of the Minnesota Poll, sponsored by the Minneapolis Tribune.

When the secret ballot (respondents mark their own ballot and put it in a ballot box carried by the interviewer) is employed with one-half of the survey sample, and the conventional interviewing procedures with the other half, it is possible to compare the results from the two groups to see if the secret ballot procedure produces a different result. Normally it does not, but on one or two occasions a difference of four or five percentage points has been found, a clear indication that a prestige factor is present.

The secret ballot has the added advantage of reducing the "undecided" vote to as little as 3 or 4 percentage points. When this residual group is examined, it is normally discovered that many will not vote. By relating the views of those who will vote to party identification, attitudes on questions, and past voting behavior, their vote can be allocated with a high degree of certainty.

        ✿   ✿   ✿

The fifth problem has to do with the timing of the final survey.

Political sentiment can and often does change during the last few days before voters go to their polling places to cast their ballots. The Gallup Poll and others learned this the hard way—in the presidential election of 1948. In that year, polling stopped about 10 to 14 days before election day. After the election, in our post-mortem investigation, we found that changes had occurred in the final days of the campaign—chiefly that Democrats who were "undecided" or who were leaning towards Dewey— went back to their 1944 voting behavior and voted for the Democratic candidate, Mr. Truman.

This experience made it imperative to find a way to conduct a final survey as late in the campaign as possible. But to achieve this goal was no small feat since interviewing has to be carried on in some states that are 2,500 miles distant from Princeton, New Jersey.

A plan was evolved that permits interviewing to be conducted Thursday, Friday, and Saturday, prior to election day. But this still leaves a two-day span when important events or campaign statements could change votes.

In two of the more recent presidential elections changes have occurred during the final days of the campaign. In 1956 the Suez Crisis and the Hungarian revolt increased the vote for Eisenhower. In 1968 President Johnson's decision, at the end of the campaign, to begin peace talks with the North Vietnamese had a measurable influence on Humphrey's vote. And there is evidence that in the British election of 1970, the report of an unfavorable trade balance in the last few days worked against Prime Minister Harold Wilson and the Labor Party.

✿   ✿   ✿

Ideally, survey findings should be programmed for the computer to produce final figures without the need to make subjective judgments, often necessary in earlier years.

An editor of a newsmagazine asks:

"The question I have always considered in need of a far better reply than those in polling have rendered to date is the extent to which human discretion determines the numbers set down in polls."

Until a polling organization has reached a point when it can, and does, program every aspect of its survey operations, it simply adds another unknown variable—personal judgment—that can increase its error.

The scientific polls do not second guess their survey figures. This practice, however, is the exception and not the rule among the private polls that often do not have the experience, the know-how, or the funds to carry out the many steps outlined here.

Sometimes the guesses of poll directors are right; more often they are wrong. One of the polls in Great Britain in the 1970 election predicted, in its final poll, a slight victory for the Conservative party. Their glory, however, was tarnished by the fact that the directors of the poll made personal judgments based upon scanty evidence.

Finally, a question posed by a West Coast political writer raises an interesting point:

"What is the next major breakthrough in polling techniques?"

A major breakthrough is not indicated. Refinements, as noted earlier, can be made, but present methods which have evolved through the years with growing experience seem to be adequate to meet present needs. And the best proof of this is the record. In terms of accuracy at the national level, improvement can be only miniscule. It is extremely doubtful that polls of the future can maintain an average error of less than 1 percentage point. More likely, the error will average 2 to 3 percentage points.

A new kind of approach to election coverage is possible, however, and could, at some point in the future, supersede the "head-to-head" approach presently used. Instead of pitting one candidate against another in the "trial heat" manner, it is possible and practical to measure political sentiment by separate measures of party strength, candidate popularity, and issue strength. A combination of these three will now produce figures almost as accurate as the standard voting preference questions presently asked. The special advantage in this approach is that no one is asked how he will vote, which candidate he prefers.

If polling organizations give up the practice of making final survey reports in campaigns in order to provide more insights into candidates and issues then this approach takes on special significance, since it meets most of the objectives of those who presently criticize poll "predictions."

Why Don't Scientific Polls Show the Same Results?

At this point, the reader should have drawn the conclusion that polling is a complicated process, involving many procedures which may vary widely from organization to organization. In fact, it is probably safe to say that no two polling organizations deal with any single aspect of polling in exactly the same way.

And this is only one of many reasons why their results often differ, and the answer to a network political commentator who asks:

"If polls are scientifically drawn, why is it that major polls are never exactly alike and sometimes contradictory?"

The layman is inclined to think of polling as a simple process, to be carried out in exactly the same way—such as making a blood count for hemoglobin in a medical laboratory. A better example, however, would be a team of engineers and scientists whose goal is to produce an airplane that will fly 1,500 miles an hour. The kind of plane developed would likely differ in many respects from a plane designed by another team working independently on this same problem. The end result might differ also: one might be able to fly 1,600 miles an hour, the other only 1,400 in actual use. Both teams obviously would be applying scientific methods.

Polling procedures differ, but so also do the questions asked. There are many facets to most social and political problems. Each poll director, therefore, must decide which are the most important and devise questions to probe those aspects accordingly. If the public is questioned on different aspects of the same general issue, findings also will differ. And this is another reason why it is so important for the poll watcher to examine carefully the exact question or questions put to the public. A poll on the problem of welfare could explore a score of facets of this problem; another poll might explore an entirely different set with understandable differences in results.

Even in fairly simple matters, poll results can differ as the questions asked the public differ. The Gallup Poll for three decades has asked this question to determine the degree of confidence in the way the president is carrying out his responsibilities

"Do you approve or disapprove of the way President (Ford) is handling his job as President?"

The Harris Poll, dealing with the same general subject, asks:

"How would you rate the job Ford is doing as president—excellent, pretty good, only fair or poor?"

In reporting these figures Harris combines the first two responses under "positive" and the last two under "negative."

Here are two ways to accomplish the same general purpose. Both questions produce meaningful results that aren't exactly the same, nor should they be.

When the questions are identical, however, and are put to the same kind of people by the same procedures and at the same time, the results are invariably within the sampling error. The Gallup Poll can supply a mountain of evidence to show that this statement is true. If it were not true, then it would be virtually impossible to measure trends. So much variation would be found that trend measurements would be meaningless. When the same questions are put on succeeding ballots, the results rarely differ by more than the expected margin of error unless an important event has intervened between the sampling periods.

The interpretation of the findings can also differ. No two social scientists, looking at the same set of raw figures, will draw exactly the same conclusion from these data. There are standards of objectivity, but it is difficult, on occasion, to know whether it is more important to stress that the bottle was "half empty," or "half full."

Throughout polling history, charges of bias have been made depending largely on whether the figures favor one side or the other. As one national committeeman points out:

> "When polls are favoring the candidate of my choice, I think they are performing a great public service, but when the reverse happens to be true, I tend to the thought that such polls are rigged, devious, and a distortion of the true picture which might well result in a complete breakdown of the democratic process."

The best protection against bias, as pointed out earlier, is to make certain that every survey report is examined carefully by persons who represent the entire range of political sentiment—from right to left. And when the sponsors of the poll also represent all shades of political belief, there is added assurance for the reader.

A Governor of a large Eastern state asks:
> "Do polls consult each other? Do they share their results?"

Obviously, each poll examines carefully the findings of other polls in the same way that the United Press International carefully eyes the reports of the Associated Press on an important news event, or that NBC or CBS would study the vote projections on election night made by each other. It is a competitive world, and every poll hopes to be more accurate than its rivals.

Except for matters that concern the field of polling as a profession, there is no consultation of the kind that leads to a change in findings or a new interpretation of results. The joint statement made by the Harris and Gallup Polls on the eve of the G.O.P. convention of 1968 in Miami was not a matter of collusion, as some have charged; it was a simple matter of a misunderstanding based upon a telephone call.

Be Wary of These Polls

The growing number of election polls sponsored by the various media and the rash of private polls taken by candidates and parties have left the public in an understandable state of confusion, particularly when poll results are contradictory.

In view of this growing welter of poll findings, the question asked by a nationally syndicated columnist should strike a responsive note:

"Just what are the criteria for an honest and professionally satisfactory poll?"

In short, which polls and polling methods merit the confidence of the poll watcher and which should be viewed with skepticism?

A list of the kinds of polls and polling methods that should be examined with caution are listed here, and for reasons that will be explained later.

The sophisticated poll watcher will be wary of:

—polls taken by telephone;

—polls taken by mail questionnaires;

—polls taken by candidates and parties or by interest groups;

—polls that are not ready to supply printed copies

of their poll findings in all elections and particularly recent ones;

—polls that do not provide a complete description of their procedures or fail to include in
each report such information as the size of the
sample, time of interviewing, exact questions
asked, the method used to reach the sample,
and the sponsor;

—polls taken in primary elections.

POLLS MADE BY TELEPHONE

Surveys made by means of telephone interviews
have increased greatly in recent years, and while this
method of conducting a survey has some advantages, it has many serious disadvantages when used to
measure political sentiment.

Questions about the reliability of this method come
from a number of persons well known in the political
world.

A Senator asks:

*"Can telephone interviewing be used in elec-
tion polling and how does personal interviewing compare with the telephone?"*

The chief advantages of the telephone method of
conducting political surveys are speed and economy.
A survey can be conducted in a single evening, and
when time is a critical factor, this is obviously an im-

portant advantage. This method is especially useful in getting first reactions of the public to an important speech or event when a high degree of accuracy is not required.

Costs are relatively low as compared with personal interviews, especially if the questionnaire or interview is a short one, limited to a few minutes.

In telephone surveys, the sample interviewed is typically made up from names in telephone books. Ingenious ways, however, have been devised to reach a sample of telephone subscribers by means of random numbers without the need to use names.

The governor of an Eastern state has discovered one of the great disadvantages of telephone polls.

"I think the credibility (of the telephone method) is questioned because of the lack of confidence in the one answering the telephone and the reluctance to discuss seriously and in depth one's convictions over the telephone."

Far greater difficulty is encountered in establishing rapport between interviewer and interviewee on the telephone than in a face-to-face situation. This shows up usually in very high "no opinion" answers, and in more refusals to be interviewed over the telephone. The easy way out for the person to answer questions concerning voting preference is to say, "I haven't made up my mind yet." It is not unusual to find the percentage of "no opinion" and "refusals" reaching

40 per cent and even higher. Skillful interviewers who have been carefully trained to deal with this problem in telephone surveys can lower the refusal rate, but seldom does the figure fall below 15 per cent.

Since it is impossible—at least at this time—to show material to the person at the other end of the telephone line, such useful techniques as the secret ballot, described earlier, or pictorial or illustrative material cannot be employed.

Another major shortcoming is noted by a Senator:

"Is telephone surveying so inherently inaccurate for pollsters as to be discredited as a scientific method? I am referring specifically to the lack of control a pollster has in a telephone interview and the discrimination of a telephone sample against poor people without telephones?"

Telephones are to be found in about 93 per cent of all homes today. Non-telephone homes are largely concentrated in the poorest areas, where the greatest percentage of non-voters is to be found. In those instances when it is important to reach all citizens of voting age, the telephone obviously discriminates, as the senator suggests, against poor people.

Telephone surveys have a built in bias toward middle and upper income groups, and older persons—

those who are more inclined to favor the Republican Party and its candidates. Usually Republican candidates score 5 per cent to 10 per cent better in telephone interviews than they would in the best personal interview surveys. Unless the poll-taker makes some correction for this factor, or changes sampling procedures, the results will reflect this bias. As a consequence, the telephone method has a poor election accuracy record in recent years.

An increasing number of persons, particularly in metropolitan areas, are asking their local telephone companies for "unlisted" numbers. In one eastern state, the proportion has reached nearly one telephone subscriber in five. Of course, by the use of random dialing, it does not make any difference whether the telephone is listed in the telephone book or not. The person's telephone will ring. That doesn't mean he is overjoyed to be called to the telephone to answer questions about his political views. As a result, the poll taker is likely to find one more person in the "no opinion" category.

Many of the disadvantages of the telephone method can be overcome by combining the personal interview method with re-interviews with the same persons by telephone.

In the course of each personal interview (made by the Gallup Poll) some twenty to thirty socio-economic facts about the person interviewed are recorded along with his telephone number. If he has no telephone this is also noted on the interviewing form.

After the forms are received at the poll headquarters in Princeton, New Jersey, a sample of the sample can easily be selected. In call-backs to the person previously interviewed, he is reminded of the interview and is told the reason for calling back by telephone. Rapport is thus easily re-established. And since all the socio-economic data needed are already available and can be punched on IBM cards, there is no need to collect this information again.

Those who do not own telephones can be taken into account by examining the data on their political behavior and preferences. Another way is to send interviewers into the poorest areas to make personal calls on a sample of non-telephone households. These can then be added, in right proportion, to the telephone interviews.

The call-back or re-interview procedure has been used on many occasions by the Gallup Poll to obtain, by telephone, the public's first reactions to major events. Subsequent personal interview surveys on the same issues reveal the general reliability of this approach.

Although the poorest accuracy record in national elections has been made by an organization using telephone interviews exclusively, improved procedures undoubtedly can eventually reduce the error factor in telephone surveys.

POLLS TAKEN BY MAIL

Strange as it may seem, in actual numbers there are probably more polls taken by mail than by any other method. The shortcomings of this method—as it is typically employed—were revealed by the Literary Digest poll in its fiasco of 1936. Yet this is the favorite polling method employed today by members of Congress.

Often, to be sure, the congressman, in seeking the views of his constituents, is more desirous of impressing those who receive the questionnaires with his eagerness to learn their views than he is with the results. However, if the returns please him, he is likely to give them to the press with the implication that they represent accurately the views of the people in his district.

A political science professor at a Midwestern university registers this complaint:

"Aren't political party leaders muddying the distinction between the professional poll and the old straw vote bunco game? Not only my congressman but the partisan press in this state send me questionnaires. The latter recently made use of the State Fair to conduct a poll."

When a congressman sends a questionnaire or ballot to every registered voter in his district, the returned ballots will contain a response bias. In surveys of this type, generally fewer than 20 per cent of all the persons who receive the ballot will bother to return them. Returns can run as high as 25 per cent but this is unusual; more likely the figure will be about 16 per cent.

Those who take the trouble to fill out and return their ballots are typically dissimilar in their views to those who fail to do so. Those who send back their marked ballots tend to be older, better educated, with higher incomes, and their views are more conservative (and more Republican) than the views of those who do not respond to mail questionnaires.

This is the reason why mail ballots have a poor election record, and provide the answer to a Midwestern national committeewoman who asks:

> *"Why are polls taken by mail inaccurate? In the past election in South Dakota, the polls showed both Democratic candidates for Congress running behind. They both won. If you do not come up with a good answer, then I fear that polls in this state will carry little weight."*

One of the ironies of polling history is that the Literary Digest had the evidence in hand to make a correct forecast in the 1936 presidential election. On the same post card ballot which asked the receiver to mark his choice for the presidency, he also was asked to check how he had voted in the previous election— 1932. When the latter figures are examined (they were published along with the figures for the 1936 candidates) it is evident that far more Republicans had marked and returned their ballots than Democrats.

Since President Roosevelt won the 1932 election with 59 per cent of the popular vote to 41 per cent for President Hoover, the returned ballots—to be representative of the nation—should have reflected this same division. The Hoover voters, however, actually outnumbered the Roosevelt voters by a good margin. By bringing poll data into line with the 1932 election returns—a simple statistical correction—the Literary Digest would have shown Roosevelt winning. The Digest, unfortunately, was committed to a policy of reporting "raw" figures and as a result it was hoist on its own petard.

Congressmen could learn an important lesson from this example. By asking on each questionnaire for additional information about the person—how he is registered (as a Democrat or Republican) and other socio-economic facts such as age, sex, education—the Congressman could obtain the data necessary to bring the sample into proper balance with known facts. This calls for guidance from persons expert in this field and a bit of courage to stand up against the charges from commentators who look upon any kind of necessary adjustment as "cooking the data."

When the sample is comprised of persons who come from a single stratum of society, the mail questionnaire is a perfectly valid method of obtaining opinions. And there are ways of testing this fact. By making a second and third and even a fourth mailing to those who do not respond to the first request, it is possible to see how the results differ with each succeeding send-out. If there is no appreciable change, then the researcher can be reasonably certain that his results contain no "response bias."

The mail questionnaire, for example, is particularly useful in obtaining the views of the leaders of a nation—persons, for example, listed in Who's Who. The cost to reach a representative sample of this group by means of personal interviewers would be prohibitive. The Gallup Poll regularly polls the county chairmen of both the Republican and Democratic parties—the local party leaders—by mail, and with great success in terms of response.

In 1970 the Gallup Poll launched a poll of world leaders. Answers of top men in government, science, business and the professions are represented in the returns which come from an amazing percentage— nearly 50 per cent of those who receive the questionnaires.

A poll of world leaders offers the opportunity to discover the major problems facing each nation of the world and to obtain the views of leaders on such international matters as population control, war, health, education, pollution, conservation, the United Nations, and efforts to improve the lot of the world's inhabitants. This new way of communicating opinions and ideas brings the hope of world peace and a world community one step closer.

POLLS TAKEN BY INTERESTED PARTIES

Virtually all research in public opinion and consumer fields can be placed in one of two categories:

1. research intended to arrive at the truth, and
2. research intended to prove a case.

If the research falls into this second category, *caveat emptor*, the reader (or buyer) beware!

It is an obvious fact of life that the candidate or party that has paid for research is not going to release findings if they show something that is regarded as damning to the cause of the sponsor. For this reason, poll findings "leaked" to the press are always suspect.

It is a ritual in political life for a candidate, or his campaign manager, to claim, as election day approaches, that he will win by a majority of XX thousands of votes. And to support this, the statement usually adds, "on the basis of our confidential polls." This puts the opposition in a hole, and the usual counter claim is that "our candidate will win by XX thousands of votes, based upon *our* polls."

━━━━━━━━━━━━━━

Few people take these claims seriously, and all of the evidence indicates that they have little or no influence in changing the views of voters. The impression is left, however, that "you can prove anything by polls." A comment on this point comes from a senator representing an Eastern state:

> "I believe professional polls are hurt by what
> I call political polls—polls taken to prove that
> a particular candidate or party is ahead. Perhaps a professional organization is needed to
> recognize those organizations that stick to sci-

entific sampling and do not become involved in partisan battles, either in their method of sampling or their news releases."

A governor of a Southern state brings up another aspect of this same problem, the misuse of polling data:

"As a candidate who has run for office in both local and state elections, one of my chief concerns is about the misuse of polls as a tactical device in such campaigns. The problem here is rather different from that on the national scene where highly reputable polls are available to prevent the serious misuse of polling information. My concern is the use of information from local polls which often is quite inaccurate and which can only be counteracted, if this is possible, by other expensive polls. What can be done to correct this situation?"

The need for a professional organization to exercise control over this situation will be dealt with later, as will the problems involved in government regulation of polls. Meanwhile, the positive values of private polling conducted for candidates and parties should be delineated.

Leaving aside "leaked" claims as to who is ahead in the polls—a practice which should be abandoned

—polls conducted by candidates and parties can be of great help to them, and even more important, to their constituents.

Properly conducted polls, as noted earlier, can improve the processes of democracy. They enable the candidate to have a better understanding of the problems which voters regard as most important. The candidate can thus address himself to the real issues of the campaign and not waste time fighting paper tigers. He can gain a better understanding of the needs of the people—all the people—and not just the clamorous minorities. In short, a carefully and honestly conducted survey should tell the candidate what his problems are, as a candidate, and should reveal, in proper perspective, the needs and problems of the voters whom he hopes to represent.

Sage advice is offered in the following statements by governors and senators who comment on their own polling experiences. The first is from a governor of a New England state.

"It is apparent to me that polling can be extraordinarily useful to a political candidate if the limitations of the technique are recognized by both the pollster and the candidate, if the polling is done in sufficient depth and over a span of time sufficient to detect the direction or trend of opinion, and if the candidate and his advisors are able to evaluate

properly and act on the information developed."

The governor of a Midwest state says:

"I have long believed that public opinion polls are of value to political leaders and those in government but good judgment must be exercised in using the results. In this connection the polling organization must share its experience with those who read the survey report to interpret the results. As you know, there is a tendency for politicians to assume that results of a survey taken at any time indicate the eventual outcome of a contest for public office. You have emphasized for many years that survey results in a political race reflect opinion only at the time the poll was taken."

A mid-Atlantic senator observes:

"From the point of view of a politician whose survival depends on a knowledge of the state of public opinion, I would venture to say that the most important thing that polls tell me is whether there is movement. It is much less significant whether an issue has or has not majority support on a given date well in advance of an election than it is that a tide of public opinion is ebbing or flowing with respect to

that candidate or issue. Under these circum-
stances, there need be less dependence on
absolute mathematical accuracy of a poll but
greater necessity for the maximum possible
number of sequential samplings."

A border state senator offers this advice:

"Political public opinion surveys are a cam-
paign tool. They should not, in my opinion . . .
over-stress head-to-head comparisons. Sur-
veys I have conducted in my campaigns are
for issue analysis and a judgment of campaign
movement. These are the areas that are usually
overlooked in political campaign survey usage
and are the areas of greatest importance."

Another New England state governor suggests a
new way that polls can help the political process:

"While it is true that in the campaigns that I
have engaged in, I have refused to be either
comforted or alarmed, as the case may be, by
the results of polls, I nevertheless believe they
have a distinct and valuable function in our
political process. Not the least of these values
is the ability of polls to increase interest among
the electorate in the issues at stake in any
given campaign."

Perhaps the strongest endorsement for the use of
private polling comes from a Mountain state senator:

"The pollsters ask more searching questions than I would. After using polls in three campaigns, I am convinced that anyone that goes into a campaign without the benefit of a poll has a serious handicap. Polls are sometimes inaccurate because the candidates look at the results and make corrections. Over the distance the polling technique must be part of every effective campaign."

The trend toward the greater use of the properly conducted private political poll is to be encouraged. Since such surveys need not cost a lot of money, especially in relation to the amounts spent foolishly for the usual campaign promotional material, they deserve to become a regular feature of American politics.

When surveys are conducted early in a campaign, they can help in planning an intelligent presentation of the candidate's and the party's viewpoints. It is not enough to know how the public stands on given issues; more important is the discovery of why voters hold the view they do. And if political campaigns are to serve their best purpose—to help educate the public on the issues—it is essential to discover just how much the public already knows.

The private and confidential poll, then, has largely served its purpose when it has helped to define the strengths and weaknesses of the candidates, brought to light the particular issues the electorate thinks are most important, and shed light on the reasons behind the public's thinking on these and other campaign issues. From such survey findings, an intelligent and effective campaign can be planned.

When candidates, or the parties they represent, use private polls merely to create what they mistakenly believe will be a bandwagon movement, they waste their money and demean the whole process of public opinion fact finding.

The Good Guys and The Bad Guys

This title is probably misleading if the reader assumes that many poll-takers deliberately falsify their poll findings. It is not a matter of honesty but of competence. And maybe of guts. The incompetent are afraid to stand behind their figures, and when the moment of truth arrives, look about for ways to protect themselves should they be "wrong."

In the case of the published polls, national or state, a simple way is available to sort out the competent from the incompetent—by their record of accuracy. It will be found that most of the better known polls have performed well; they make every effort to use the best methods since their prestige depends on being close to the mark in elections.

It is in the field of private political polling that one finds new and inexperienced practitioners—some who use methods that have recognized shortcomings; others who do not know how to interpret and to apply their findings. It is chiefly these novices who give the profession a bad reputation. A candidate who is assured that he is certain to win and then loses is not likely to become an avid believer in polls, and this happens all too often.

On the other hand, the candidate who uses polls only to discover whether he is ahead or behind in the race is almost certain to be disillusioned sooner or later.

A Midwestern governor, who apparently has been in this position, makes this wry comment:

"I have little credence in polls. If they say I am ahead, I cannot afford to believe them. If they say I am behind, I cannot afford to believe them."

Every polling organization, both public and private, should be willing to supply printed copies of its results in the elections in which it has conducted polls, and particularly in the most recent ones. These reports should reveal the final survey findings published before the election, not claims made afterward. In the case of television or radio polls, transcripts should be made available of the last pre-election broadcast in which poll figures were announced.

If a polling organization is unwilling to make these reports available to individuals who have good reason to request them, then it is justifiable to assume that the organization has something to hide.

As stated earlier, the average error or deviation from absolute accuracy is the best test of the procedures and methods employed by a polling organization in election surveys. Since a poll can be on target in one election and far off in the next, the record which covers many elections is the best standard for judging its excellence.

The deviation, it should be pointed out, can be determined only if the poll reports its final figures without the "undecided" vote. There is always a temptation after the election to claim that the undecided group went this way or that way—to make the poll look better. In fact, the very size of this group is a good indication of whether the poll has followed the best polling techniques. In the final days of a political campaign, the undecided vote can be reduced to a very few percentage points by the proper procedures. Many of those who still remain undecided actually do not vote and the remaining few can be allocated without resort to subjective judgments, as pointed out earlier.

The undecided vote offers a convenient excuse to justify a wrong forecast as a network commentator opines:

> *"Rightly or wrongly, I have the impression the poll-takers can use the undecided vote after the election as a scapegoat for their failures."*

A professor at a Southern university asks this question:

> *"How valid are the claims of the 'last minute switches' or decisions made by the undecided that are frequently used by pollsters when they blow an election? Is this speculation or is there really supportive evidence?"*

When the undecided group is large, it is usually made up of many persons who are reluctant to tell interviewers what their voting intentions and preferences are. A few will be found who are on the fence, unable to make up their minds, but as noted earlier, a high proportion of these do not get to the polls. As a general principle, the undecided tend to return to their normal voting pattern established in earlier elections. But this is something that must be ascertained anew in each election.

Since its establishment, the Gallup Poll has always published final survey figures that can be checked against election returns. The size of the undecided group is always reported, but final figures are published that exclude this figure. The complete record, covering some 20 national elections since 1936, will be found in the appendix.

A widely syndicated newspaper columnist asks this very pertinent question:

"If pollsters are not in the prediction business why do they make such a big thing out of their accuracy as supported by elections?"

In both print and broadcast media the public is constantly reminded that polls were wrong in 1948, in many primary elections, and in the British election of 1970 with the obvious inference that all of their findings should be suspect. Strangely, no article has yet appeared in any newspaper or magazine that reports or analyzes the complete record of polls since 1935, and more particularly polling experience since 1948.

The public needs to be warned about possible errors in polling; the public is also entitled to know all the facts about polling accuracy.

Polls in Primary Elections

The record of polls in primary elections is so bad that the sophisticated poll watcher will pay little attention to them, or make allowance for large errors, if he does.

Primary elections pose all of the problems met in a national election, and, as pointed out earlier, require a sample of the same size and of the same high quality. The fact that a state has a population only a fraction of that of the whole nation makes little difference.

The task of eliminating non-voters in primary elections is more difficult for the very simple reason that a much smaller proportion of voters takes the trouble to vote in primaries than in general elections. In some states as few as 10 per cent of all voters cast their ballots in primary elections.

Last minute statements and events are much more likely to influence voters than in national elections when the choice is between a well known candidate of one party, and an equally well known candidate of the opposing party.

Finally, in primary elections the party machine can exert its greatest power. By turning out the party faithful when other voters are staying home, the machine can garner enough votes to give the favored party candidate a marked advantage.

The question that the polling organization must answer is this: Is surveying in a primary election worth the extra time, money, and effort required?

The planning, staff requirements, sample size and costs of polling in a single state primary—if a high degree of accuracy is to be maintained—are at least as great as those for a national election.

At the present time, the polls taken in primary elections are little better than "pilot" studies—mere straws in the wind—and no one should regard them as anything else.

Polling Costs and Competition

Because of its importance to government and to the people, the assessment of public opinion on the major issues of the day should attract dozens of research organizations. Unfortunately, this is not the case. Since modern polling was introduced in 1935, there has never been a time when more than three organizations were reporting results regularly on a national basis. And for much of this time, only two have been operating at the national level. The Gallup Poll is the only organization that spans the entire period from the beginning. On the other hand, research organizations dealing with consumer attitudes and opinions now number in the hundreds. In New York City alone, a total of 364 research organizations are listed in the telephone directory. More than 50 organizations that specialize in private election polling were listed by the National Journal.[1] Since most market or consumer research organizations will undertake polls for candidates and parties, the number of companies that do research in this field probably numbers at least 1,000.

The reasons why there are so few organizations in the field of national public opinion polling are not hard to find. Of all fields of research, polling

[1]National Journal, August 14, 1971

on public issues is the least profitable. In fact, no organization, including the Gallup Poll, could maintain its present staff and facilities without engaging in other kinds of research. The money that is paid by sponsoring newspapers, in the case of the Gallup Poll, hardly meets the out-of-pocket expenses for this work.

Another reason why so few firms have entered the field of public opinion is the fear of having to go through elections and being "put on the spot" to deliver accurate election reports. Dr. Henry Durant, founder of the British Institute of Public Opinion, has described this situation in a colorful way. In a speech before a group of university students, he had this to say:

"My advice to all would-be election forecasters is to think again. It is the most stupid job you can ever take up, no matter how hard you try to find a worse one. If you get the election right, everyone takes it for granted. If you get it wrong, you are standing alone and utterly ashamed, and there is nothing you can do about it."

It would be difficult to find any other profession whose leaders are held publicly accountable for their actions in quite the same way. However, it is the awful penalties for being "wrong" that have spurred the development of research procedures. As a result, in no other field of the social sciences has the prediction of human behavior reached the same high level of accuracy.

Politics being what it is in the United States, the party whose candidate is lagging behind feels compelled to claim that the polling organization reporting this unpleasant fact is applying discredited methods, has too small a sample, is "cooking" its figures, or is failing to reach some segment of the population that favors the losing candidate. So-called experts can always be found to lend credence to these charges by insisting that better methods are available, although not one of them has ever proved this in an election test. The real knock-out blow is supposed to be the 1948 election when all polls arrived at the wrong answer. The impression the critics hope to leave with voters is that 1948 is the only election in which polls were ever taken up to the present time.

However, this is all part of the game of politics and unless one is ready to get an occasional kick in the shin, he should not take up polling.

So, maybe it isn't too difficult to understand why only two or three polling organizations are carrying on the work of assessing and reporting public opinion at the national level.

These deterrents, it should be emphasized, apply only to the polls that are reported to the general public through the medium of the press and the broadcast media. Private or confidential polls are not exposed to the critics; such polls can charge what the traffic will bear and they are seldom held accountable for their errors. They may, of course, lose a client if they perform badly; but then there are many other buyers who are not well enough informed about polling matters to distinguish good research from bad research.

Present day costs of polling are considerable, and because funds available to candidates and parties are always limited, it is natural that they should look for polling methods and procedures that fit their budgets.

A national committeeman comments:

"Many times during my service as a state chairman we had need of guidance in state legislative districts and congressional districts. The budget of local candidates involved would not permit professional polling. How can we get some guidance on issues and candidates at a price that can be afforded?"

This same point of view is echoed by the mayor of an Eastern city.

"A major problem for a candiadate for minor office—mayor, for example, is that the services of a reliable poll man cannot be afforded."

The relatively high cost of taking polls that employ the best methods has led many persons in public life to sacrifice reliability for money considerations.

For example, a national committeeman in a West Coast state makes this comment:

> *"Accuracy is a function of money. Polls are like automobiles. With 300 interviews on the telephone at $10 each (or $3,000) we can get a quick idea of where we are. We can find out if anyone really cares about mental health cutbacks. Or, with 1,000 personal interviews in the home at $20 each (or $20,000) we can get some pretty good statistics on what the machinist's wife in Dayton thinks. In many cases the former is adequate."*

The problem then, for many office holders, is how to reduce polling costs without sacrificing too much in the way of quality.

The governor of a large Eastern state asks, almost wistfully:

> *"Can polling costs be reduced? There would be a great deal more of it if the cost could be brought down. For example, I would like to know very much what the citizens of my state are thinking of our administration, our efforts to introduce economy and efficiency, our new programs, etc. I can't in fairness impose upon the taxpayers the cost of such a poll, even though I know that it could make a constructive contribution to better government."*

Misreading the public's mind about needs and goals can cost governments millions of dollars. The present state of mind of legislators, however, is that it is better to waste these millions making or correcting mistakes than to spend a few thousand dollars taking soundings in advance that would enable them to make wiser decisions.

Another aspect of this problem of the constructive use of polling results is emphasized by a leading opinion analyst. After many years of experience in dealing with polls and public opinion, he has reached this conclusion:

"I am more convinced than ever that it is imperative that there be a reliable program of public opinion assessment and reporting in this country. The influence of television, with its insatiable appetite for the sensational and bizarre, creates a distorted impression of the character of public attitudes and values and it is very important, in my view, that a truly representative report of these attitudes should be available. Public opinion is an increasingly important factor in the nation's decisions and we must have a dependable source of information about it."

The need for a dependable source of information about the public's thinking on issues of the day applies not only to the federal government but to state and city governments as well. In a few states highly reliable polling organizations perform this function. And, in at least one city, Dayton, Ohio, an important experiment has been funded by the Kettering Foundation to see how polling data can help local leaders by shedding light on the opinions and needs of residents of this area.

Public officials, at all levels, to function effectively, require a reliable "play-back" mechanism that will inform them about the reaction of the electorate to their programs, reforms that will meet greater acceptance, areas of resistance, and of equal importance, the state of public knowledge about what is being done and why.

In two states, Iowa and Minnesota, leading newspapers, the Des Moines Register and Tribune and the Minneapolis Tribune, support highly competent public opinion research organizations that deal not only with state issues but national issues as well. In three or four other states—California, Texas, Michigan— equally competent organizations carry on polls on issues of the day for newspapers and other media.

University survey research centers—notably Michigan and Chicago—have performed a needed and highly valuable service in dealing with the special concerns of government agencies and foundations.

The argument is sometimes advanced that if polling is important to the democratic process, the government should assume this responsibility. Actually, the government now supports the largest polling organization in the world. The Bureau of the Census polls the nation monthly to obtain information on a wide variety of subjects, including employment. The Department of Health, Education, and Welfare sponsors scores of surveys as does nearly every department of government.

Gerald Ford and his predecessors, going back to Franklin D. Roosevelt, have all had survey information available to them. A regular flow of polling data goes into the White House on many aspects of the political scene, not only from the public polls but from private polling organizations.

So, the question is not whether the government should poll, or sponsor polls, but whether it should conduct polls on political, economic, and social issues of the day not for private, but for public consumption.

The problems, however, that would have to be resolved if the government attempted to do what the privately financed and unofficial polls are presently doing would be colossal. Almost certainly a government polling agency would be placed under constant pressure to produce the "right" figures, and if the "right" figures were not forthcoming, funds to carry on the work might be cut off or reduced. Each political party would find it imperative to know, in advance, what each poll on a given issue would likely show, and be ready to refute the findings. A small army of "experts" would be hired by the political parties and by pressure groups to prove that any question wording was faulty, if the results displeased them.

An independent agency, supported by government funds, would have almost as many problems. The same criticisms would be aimed at such an agency as those directed at present polling organizations.

Most important, however, would be the assumption that since the government supplied the money and the guidance, the results should be regarded as official, and consequently followed to the letter. This would allow little latitude for legislative or executive action. Only by instituting official referendums —as in the case of Switzerland—could or should results assume the character of a true mandate to be religiously followed.

For the foreseeable future, therefore, the assessing and reporting of public opinion are probably best left to persons and organizations that have no connection with parties or candidates, that obtain their financial support from groups or sources that are not committed to any single political or ideological viewpoint, that have neither a conservative nor a liberal orientation, and whose findings can be regarded as reliable but not "official."

Self Regulation Versus Government Regulation

The effort to bring a measure of self regulation into the field of polling was initiated some years ago by the individuals who introduced modern polling in the mid-thirties. In the year 1968, an organization was formed which later assumed the name, National Council on Published Polls. The first president was Archibald M. Crossley, one of the pioneers in the field of public opinion polling. In 1970 he was followed by Richard Scammon, Director, Elections Research Center, and then by Robert Bower, Director of the Bureau of Social Science Research. The present head of this group is Albert H. Cantril.

One of the accomplishments to date of this group has been to draw up a set of standards for published polls. These standards apply not only to the factual data that must be included in every report of poll or survey findings, but also to the disclosure of other information about research procedures, sponsors, and other pertinent facts.

Members who belong to the NCPP are few in number, and for the most part have observed these standards in the past. Unfortunately, the polls that engage in questionable practices are not eager to join such an organization and be subject to its discipline. Moreover, no way has been found, up to this time, to establish control over the scores of private or confidential polls. Unfortunately, it is chiefly these polls, with their contradictory claims, that confuse the public.

The American Association for Public Opinion Research, established in 1947, includes all persons in academic, polling, and marketing fields who have an interest in the public opinion field.

A committee of this parent group has adopted a set of standards for polling that is essentially the same as those laid down by the NCPP.

Specifically, these standards call for the inclusion of these facts in every survey report:

1. a description of the sample reached,
2. the method employed for reaching the sample,
3. the size of the sample,
4. the exact wording of the questions asked,
5. the time of the interviewing.

When polls are "leaked" to the press, the survey organization has a duty to report the full findings if the facts released do not give an accurate account of the over-all results.

Both organizations have difficulty in enforcing their standards. Even public reprimand or dismissal is not a very serious threat. Moreover, present laws make such actions subject to libel suits if the accused party wishes to pursue the matter in the courts.

―――――――――

No one has seen the problem more clearly than a political writer for a large Eastern newspaper, who observes:

"Unfortunately, I am afraid that as long as driven people (the politician, the pollster, and the press) make up the political process, there are going to be politicians ordering polls to support pre-determined campaign tactics, pollsters who are willing to go along with this, and the press that is willing to print it. One hope, possibly, is for some sort of a Better Business Bureau that a reporter could refer to at least to get some idea of whether the poll being leaked to him at least meets general standards of accuracy and competency . . . I wish, of course, that a similar self-policing organization might be possible among reporters and politicians."

As the writer points out, the problem of regulating polls involves not only all polls, both public and private, but the press and politicians—a task of gargantuan proportions.

In the field of polling, it is difficult to establish a professional group committed to a given set of standards, chiefly because anyone can take a poll and, it might be added, does,—there are street corner polls, state fair polls, coupon in the paper polls, bubble gum polls, grain bag polls, supermarket polls, television audience polls.

Hope of establishing standards that will be widely followed lies mainly with the press. If political commentators and writers are well enough informed about methods to distinguish between properly and objectively conducted polls and those that are poorly designed or conducted for political advantage, then the public they reach will be less inclined to treat all polls alike.

The first step in separating the sheep from the goats is to discover how willing the polling organization is to provide full information about its procedures, its history and its accuracy, its sources of income, and the training and background of those in charge of the research.

This information should be available, but one restriction must be observed. On occasion, in past election campaigns, individuals who request information about methods and procedures and other pertinent facts have little interest in this information per se. They hope desperately to find something that will discredit the poll's current findings, which are obviously galling to them. A distorted account of the poll's procedures and accuracy invariably results. For this reason, certain restraints must be imposed, and requests for information must come in proper form and for proper reasons.

One of the chief criticisms of polls made by legislators and students of polling is the reporting of poll results during election campaigns, showing in figures which candidate is ahead. It is logical, therefore, that they should suggest that one of the practices which should be eliminated by a professional organization is the custom of reporting the standing of candidates.

This suggestion is phrased in these words by a Senator representing an Eastern state:

"Should recognized pollsters consider policing themselves by refusing to publish or allow to be published, head-to-head figures prior to election day? . . . Published polls should be confined to voter sentiment on the issues."

The arguments, pro and con, on this point have been dealt with at some length in earlier chapters. Suffice it to say here that cogent reasons can be advanced for using polling facilities chiefly for the purpose of diagnosis rather than prognosis.

Bills have been introduced in Congress regularly since the 1920's to regulate polls, as noted earlier. Insofar as these suggested laws require polling organizations to disclose their methods and to include in printed or broadcast reports the kind of information needed by readers to interpret poll findings in an intelligent way, they would definitely benefit the public and the polling profession.

However, problems of a constitutional nature, encountered by such laws, would almost certainly rule them out. Poll reports differ from the reports of political writers and commentators only in their use of figures. Words can convey virtually the same facts, but perhaps without the same authority.

A one-man poll, done carefully and on the basis of much experience, can produce a reliable estimate of public opinion, as demonstrated by the able political analyst, Samuel Lubell.

To avoid conflict with the constitutional right of free speech and of a free press, Congress and the courts would have a nigh impossible task of trying to draw a distinction between a purportedly systematic attempt to gauge sentiment, as opposed to one that might be employed by a political observer.

President Truman once declared that he did not need a public opinion poll to find out how people felt about an issue. All he had to do, Mr. Truman asserted, was "to go out and to talk to the people." He was right. And, it might be added, this is exactly what a survey organization does. The only real difference is that a polling organization attempts to do in a planned and systematic way what Mr. Truman did in a casual way.

The argument that poll results influence voters (a point dealt with at length earlier) could be countered by saying that the polls are not unique in this respect, even granting what the evidence fails to show—that they do have some influence. In the United States we accept that it is proper, even useful, for a newspaper to try to influence its readers to vote for certain candidates, without giving the opposing candidates a full and fair opportunity to rebut the arguments in the same editorial space. And it is recognized as perfectly proper for well known persons in professional and educational fields to buy newspaper advertising space to try to influence voters to follow their own choices of candidates. Why, then, it could be argued in the courts, is it not equally proper to let the public know what their fellow citizens think, through the medium of polls?

If legal restraints were placed upon poll results that show one candidate ahead of another, a way would be found to convey this information to voters through the various media, by saying that it is based on "scientific evidence" without even mentioning the word "poll."

Proposals to prohibit by law the publication of poll results near the end of election campaigns have been introduced in the parliaments of three or four nations, among them Great Britain. Former Prime Minister Harold Wilson takes a sensible view of such proposals. He makes this point in the Britannica Book of the Year (1971):

> "Disenchantment with the polls has revived proposals that the publication of poll results should be forbidden by law for a given period before an election. This was actually recommended by the all-party Speaker's conference on electoral reform a few years ago, but on the government's advice the House of Commons rejected it. It is unlikely to occur. For one thing, private polls would continue to be taken; rumours about their results would circulate and might even lead to speculation on security markets."

The likely result of banning election polls in Great Britain, as indicated by Mr. Wilson, would undoubtedly be duplicated in the United States.

The hope, therefore, to correct such abuses as exist must rest with the polling profession itself, aided and abetted by the media and their political writers and commentators. Also, the Fair Campaign Practices Committee, which presently exercises restraints on candidates, can be of great help by curbing the misuse of polling data by candidates for political office.

A detailed account of the Nedzi bill, introduced in Congress by Congressman Lucien Nedzi, calling for full disclosure of polling procedures and sponsorship will be found in a later chapter.

Polling Accuracy

In most elections, a few polls find their results wide of the mark. It is only the elections in which all polls are on the "wrong" side that create a furor and are remembered:

A professor at an Eastern university asks:

"What causes the famous errors in predicting election outcomes such as the Truman-Dewey race and the Harold Wilson-Edward Heath contest in England?"

A writer for a leading journal asks this further question:

"Do polls need to re-examine their methodology in view of their disastrous experience in the 1970 British elections? What is the explanation for that fiasco?"

The simple answer to the errors registered in both these elections is that polling methods and procedures were not adequate for the task. They do have to be re-examined in Great Britain just as they were thoroughly re-examined after the 1948 election in the United States. And as a general principle, it might be added that methodology should be re-examined after every election.

Actually, the experiences in these two elections, traumatic as they were to the poll-takers, proved to be blessings in disguise. It is the nature of man to resist making drastic changes until some bitter experience forces him to do so.

Every election is different. New factors arise or old ones operate in a different manner. Consequently, new procedures must be found or old ones improved. The successful application of methods in one election, in short, is no guarantee that these same methods will work successfully in the next one.

This means that the poll-taker must always be on the alert for new factors, and must devise early warning systems whenever this is possible. Unfortunately, the new factors are often brought to light only in the post-mortems held after wrong predictions have been made.

In the Truman-Dewey race in 1948, poll-takers assumed that a change in standing of candidates in a presidential race was unlikely to occur in the final days of a campaign. In fact, they had not devised an efficient way to get ballots back from distant states by ordinary mail and to tabulate them in fewer than 10 days. Anything that happened in this 10-day period to affect the standing of the candidates could not be reflected in the final survey figures. Ways were subsequently found to interview voters within a couple of days of the election.

Only a few years later, this new system saved the Gallup Poll from making a sizeable error in the 1956 race between Eisenhower and Stevenson. During the last 10 days, the Hungarian revolt and the Suez crisis had an important impact on Eisenhower's strength, lifting it percentagewise by almost the same amount as the error registered in 1948. The strong trend toward Humphrey in the final month of the 1968 campaign could only have been measured accurately by nationwide soundings taken at regular intervals up to a couple of days of the election.

It was not only the time factor in the 1948 election that proved the undoing of the polls. Many other shortcomings were brought to light in the agonizing reappraisal following that election. It became evident that samples had to be improved, that better ways had to be devised for dealing with the undecided vote. In the same type of re-examination undertaken in later elections, the need to have better ways to screen out non-voters, and to deal with intensity and prestige factors became evident. Measures have been taken to deal with these factors, and with demonstrable success.

The British polls failed to take full advantage of American experience under the assumption that elections in Great Britain involve factors different from those found in U.S. elections. As it turned out, the 1970 failure of the polls in the Wilson-Heath contest was almost exactly a replay of the 1948 experience in the United States.

Progress in polling, as in other fields, comes from taking full advantage of experience, and from experiments initiated to find new and better methods.

By following this program, the Gallup Poll has

been able to show steady progress from early days, as measured in terms of the average deviation between poll results and election returns.

In the period beginning with the election of 1936 and covering the seven succeeding national elections (presidential and congressional) the average deviation of final survey results from the actual division of the popular vote in the election itself was 4.0 percentage points.

The 1950 and 1952 elections were used by the Gallup Poll to develop new methods to correct the faults of the 1948 race, especially the problem of the undecided vote, the problem of turnout, and polling up to election time. In the period beginning with the election of 1954 through 1965—a period embracing six elections—the average deviation was 1.6 percentage points. In the last four elections, the average error has been 0.8 percentage points.

It would be unrealistic, however, to assume that the record of the last three elections can be maintained in the future.

If we look back over the last nine elections, we find that in two the errors were larger than 2.5 percentage points. It is well to have in mind that sampling error is not the only source of error in an election survey. Error is introduced in the process of identifying voters and non-voters, by how the undecided ultimately vote, by last minute trends, by party activity.

Therefore, it can be expected that polls will be wrong, on occasion, in future elections. Improvements in methods will continue to be made which will reduce, but never eliminate, error.

So the question asked by a national committee-man answers itself:

"Will the time ever come when polls will be so accurate that we do not need to hold elections?"

That time will never come because with the same certainty that it can be said that polls will be right most of the time, it can also be said that they will be wrong on occasion.

A completely different approach to the appraisal of political strength is possible without reporting the head-to-head standings of the candidates, following the usual practice. This involves independent measurements of party strength, candidate popularity, and issue strength—the three chief factors determining voting preference. This new approach, admittedly, does not provide the same kind of precise information as present methods that reveal exactly how a candidate is faring against his opponent.

However, when the time comes, as it likely will, when polling organizations concentrate on diagnosis in election campaigns rather than prognosis, and give up the usual head-to-head standings of the candidates, which rouse the most venomous criticism of polls, it will still be possible to show which candidate is doing better and at the same time shed far more light on the "why."

A national committeewoman, representing a Southern state, asks:

"What kind of accuracy do you have on your overall results? And how about the accuracy of the major-subgroups such as geographic regions and economic groups?"

Election figures are not reported by such sub-groups as "economic," "educational," "religious," etc. It can be presumed, however, that if the national poll figures are highly accurate, then the figures for sub-groups are likely to be reasonably correct.

It is possible, on the other hand, to measure polling accuracy by geographic regions, since these figures are readily available from election returns. Typically, the Gallup Poll reports figures for two areas—South and non-South.

Final survey figures are published in the sponsoring newspapers on the Sunday or Monday before election day. The record, therefore, can be checked by anyone who wishes to do so, along with the text of accompanying final reports. In each instance, final figures have been reported in a way to enable anyone to measure the accuracy of the final survey results.

This means that the undecided vote has always been allocated. Too many polling organizations, to avoid being put on the spot with survey results that they fear may miss the mark, leave in a sizeable group of the "undecided." As noted earlier, this offers an easy escape hatch.

The deviation of survey results from actual election returns are based upon the division of the popular vote. In off-year or congressional elections, the division is based upon the total vote cast for Democratic and Republican candidates for the 435 seats in the House of Representatives, this being the only national contest in off-year elections. The latter type of election is the type found in nations where parliamentary majorities decide which party wins. In many ways, these elections are more complicated and difficult from a researcher's point of view than elections in which two or three well known candidates head their respective party tickets.

The election record provides evidence to answer the charges sometimes made that the "X" poll has a Democratic or Republican bias. A built-in bias would almost certainly reveal itself in election survey results, since this is the evidence used by the critics to charge bias. Of course, any kind of bias—intentional or otherwise—would add still another error factor, and a poll that is jealous of its record of accuracy would be insane to let any kind of bias complicate further its many problems.

In the case of the Gallup Poll, it will be noted

from the accuracy record that in the last eleven elections the final Gallup estimates of the Democratic percentage averaged 0.2 percentage points higher than the true figure. In six of the eleven elections the Gallup estimate was slightly more Democratic than the election result; in five it was slightly more Republican.

Throughout this book, the point has been stressed that polls can be expected to be highly accurate most of the time, but until the laws of probability are nullified, large errors are certain to be registered on occasion, errors that arise from the sampling process and from other sources.

Very substantial errors can be expected in primary elections and in fact, in many types of elections when turnout of voters is low. Especially is this true when one segment of the population is vitally concerned whereas other large segments are indifferent or only mildly interested. School bond issues often fall into this category; also, issues that affect the elderly or that apply particularly to one religious or racial group. A vote on providing financial help to parochial schools almost certainly will induce a high proportion of Catholics to cast their ballots and unless polling techniques are efficient in separating those who will bother to vote from those who will not, the poll can register a substantial error. Elections of this type involve not only a differential turnout, but often prestige factors as well. Those who care little about the outcome of the vote, will not exert any extra effort to vote on election day.

One of the wisest observations about polling accuracy comes from Professor Richard Rose of the Department of Politics of the University of Strathclyde, Glasgow. In a post-election analysis of the 1970 British experience, he writes:

"In political surveys, as in many other forms of human endeavor, the choice is not between total knowledge and total ignorance, but rather between more or less knowledge, or more or less accuracy. People who wish for a sure thing, whether on a general election, a stock market share, or a doctor's diagnosis, should not consult professionally qualified men, but rather soothsayers, astrologers, or others who make a living by taking money from those who believe that perfect knowledge is possible."

The Public Opinion Referendum

James Bryce regarded the referendum as the ideal way of discovering the public's views on specific issues.

> "It is the logical recourse, but it is troublesome and costly to take the votes of millions of people over an area so large as that of one of the greater states; much more, then, is this difficult to apply in federal matters."

Through a new plan worked out and tested in the 1970 election, Bryce's objections based upon costs and trouble can be largely overcome. The "public opinion referendum" which relies upon a different type of sampling, provides a useful procedure to employ in assessing public opinion on issues at all levels of government—local, state, and national.

The procedure does not in any sense supplant regular sampling surveys of the type conducted during the last three decades. Rather, the new system parallels and complements the survey method.

The chief advantage of the referendum system is that it more closely resembles the election process itself and is, therefore, more easily understood by the typical citizen. Moreover, individuals conducting the referendum need not have the technical training necessary to undertake sample surveys.

The referendum system is a product of three devclopments. The first goes back to 1938 and to an experiment with "barometer" counties. Erie County, Ohio, had mirrored the political tides of the nation for many decades, and in August of that year the Gallup Poll conducted a special survey to see how the residents of this county compared in their views with the views of the whole nation.

The second step was taken in April, 1949, in a project involving a city-wide referendum on eleven issues—local, state, and national. This undertaking, described as "Experiment in Democracy" was conducted in New Brunswick, New Jersey, in cooperation with the New Brunswick Home News. An impressive number, 7,232 voters, in this many households, participated in the experiment. In terms of families casting ballots, participation was greater than in most elections in that city.

The third step was an exhaustive analysis of the barometer approach. This involved a study of the voting history of every county in the United States in many presidential elections, to identify those that have reflected accurately the shift in political tides. These counties were then in turn examined for current factors that might render them less accurate as barometer areas at the present time.

Barometer counties sooner or later fail to be an accurate guide to political trends. Their claim, of course, must rest upon past performance. So the need is great to analyze the racial, religious, and economic composition of the county to see that factors, such as these, will not make them less representative when a new assessment of public opinion is to take place.

To take account of sectional differences the safest course is to choose counties that are representative not of the whole nation, but of their own region.

Analysis of the voting history of the 3,068 counties in the United States reveals that in all major regions of the nation, counties can be selected that meet these many tests.

Using the experience of the most recent presidential elections, counties that have voted within 3 percentage points of the actual Democratic-Republican division of the presidential vote in three successive presidential years have about an equal chance of being within 3 percentage points in the next election.

For example, roughly half of those counties that reflected national sentiment within 3 percentage points in the presidential years of 1952, 1956, and 1960 came within 3 percentage points of the national division of the vote in 1964. And about half of the counties that were within 3 percentage points of the national figure in the elections of 1956, 1960 and 1964 came within 3 percentage points of the correct percentage of the winning candidate in 1968.

When counties that fail to meet the tests for current representativeness are eliminated, then the number that come within 3 percentage points is substantially increased. In fact, two out of three of the remaining "indicator" counties are within the 3 percentage point error mark.

The first opportunity to try the new referendum approach on a national scale came in the fall of 1970. James Karayn, Chief of the Washington Bureau of National Educational Television, became interested in this new way to assess national opinion, particularly since it provided a more realistic and a more exciting way to give viewers an understanding of the political forces at work throughout the nation.

Four counties were selected, each with a record of accurately reflecting the sentiment of its area in the last four presidential elections. New London County, Connecticut, was selected to represent the Eastern section of the nation; Shelby County, Tennessee, the South; Montgomery County, Illinois, the Midwest, and San Luis Obispo County, California, the West.

Since it is impractical to undertake a referendum that reaches all residents of a county, using the same principle again as that employed in the original selection, smaller units were chosen within the county which together reflected the county figures. In this manner a referendum becomes manageable, and yet produces enough cases to provide a reliable result for the county.

The next step is to cover every household within the selected districts. In the New Brunswick, New Jersey test, newsboys were used to deliver the referendum ballots and to collect them. In the 1970 referendum, this role was performed by news carriers and Boy Scouts. The referendum ballots were delivered to all households within carefully selected precincts and collected on succeeding days.

In the referendum plan, each person who receives a ballot is assured that his views will be held in strict confidence. Each ballot is sealed in an envelope before it is collected. No identifying marks are placed on the envelope, except the district number, to permit ballots to be tabulated district by district.

In one county (New London, Connecticut) as many as 1247 ballots were returned from a total of 1713 distributed, or 73 per cent. Eight of the 26 Norwich Bulletin newsboys who worked on the project collected over 90 per cent of the ballots they had distributed in their districts.

In the four indicator counties, the total return was 55 per cent, a figure which compares favorably with actual voting turnout of less than 50 per cent in the 1970 election.

The number of marked and returned ballots is a function not of interest but of organization at the local level. It is entirely possible in future tests of this type to increase returns to 70 per cent and above.

Ten questions or "propositions" were included on the referendum ballot. The voter was asked to check the appropriate box. Issues in the 1970 Referendum included withdrawal of troops from Vietnam, lowering the voting age, making marijuana legal, speeding up integration, improving the living conditions of the poor, law enforcement, school busing, requiring automobiles to be equipped with anti-pollution devices, wage and price controls, and student riots.

The referendum has many special advantages. At the national level, sentiment of the whole nation can be reflected by a careful selection of counties, and districts within these counties. Results should closely parallel those obtained by the survey method, or for that matter, an official nationwide referendum.

At the state level, issues that might be placed on official election ballots can be presented to voters in selected districts which mirror the voting habits of the state—and at far less cost and trouble. This type of approach can serve as an excellent citizen feedback system to elected officials, both state and federal.

The referendum system is particularly useful at the local level. In towns and cities of 40,000 or less, a public opinion referendum can cover the whole city. In cities larger than this, as noted above, districts can be chosen on the basis of their past voting record and their present representativeness.

The referendum system involves many persons, and one of its virtues is that it does not require a highly trained staff. It is a do-it-yourself operation that permits many individuals to participate in the democratic process.

The public opinion referendum might well supplant the questionnaires mailed out by many representatives and senators to voters in their home districts and states. Local or state committees could decide upon the issues to include in the referendum—on a non-partisan or bi-partisan basis—and the wording of questions could be agreed upon by the opposing groups.

The results of such a referendum would offer a far more accurate assessment of public opinion than the present mail ballots sent out by congressmen, and the overall costs would be no greater.

And certainly by participating in the planning, distribution, and tabulation of the ballots, voters would take much more interest in the findings, and the political process itself should become more realistic and meaningful.

The Nedzi Truth in Polling Act

A thorough investigation of polls, and particularly their use in election periods, was conducted by a Congressional committee under the chairmanship of Cong. Lucien N. Nedzi. The hearings were held in Washington during September, 1972.

The hearings were held in connection with a bill introduced by Congressman Nedzi and described as a Truth in Polling Act. The bill would require polling organizations to file with the Library of Congress, within a period of 72 hours after publication, the results of any published poll dealing with any election for Federal office or with any political issue. In addition, the following information would be required to be filed at the same time: the name of the poll's sponsor, the nature of the sample, the size of the sample, the method of reaching respondents, the completion rate, the time of interviewing, and the exact questions asked.

The Washington investigation was both comprehensive and constructive. The hearings were conducted by Congressman Nedzi in an eminently fair manner with the goal of trying to arrive at disclosure policies that would not violate the First Amendment and still would serve the purposes of the public, the media, and the polling organizations concerned.

Virtually every individual who has taken a prominent role in public opinion research in the United States testified during the hearings and offered his views as to how best to deal with the problems and the abuses occurring, on occasion, in this field.

Basically, the bill would require the same kind of disclosure of polling procedures called for in the standards established by the National Council on Published Polls and the American Association for Public Opinion Research.

The writer testified in support of the Nedzi bill. I did so because the major thrust of the Act was to give legal force to disclosure requirements that voluntary compliance does not ensure.

Self regulation is to be preferred always as opposed to government regulation, and that is the chief reason why I initiated the founding of the National Committee on Published Polls and its standards. However, in a field in which professional education and training can not be insisted upon, with the result that anyone can launch a poll for any purpose, good or bad, and with any kind of procedures, good or bad, it seems advisable to protect the public's interest by the disclosure of a few basic facts about a poll's operation and sponsorship.

In one important respect, the bill, in my opinion, did not go far enough in its disclosure requirements. This has to do with a poll's history and its performance. The public has a right to know in which polls it can place some measure of confidence, and a poll's election record provides virtually the only objective evidence on this score.

Senator Charles E. Goodell of New York, who had made a thorough study of polls, and had, in fact, introduced a bill in the Senate in 1970 covering much the same ground as the Nedzi bill, states the case this way:

"Despite the silence of the professional standards on disclosure of pollsters' records, the professionals agree that this would be an item of information probably most useful for the typical voter in conducting his own nonprofessional assessment of published poll results. The Act (Sen. Goodell's) seeks disclosure of the average percentage error, during the preceding five years, of the final pre-election surveys conducted by a researcher."

Since only one or two elections might have been covered by a poll in a five-year period, I would suggest that the entire record of the polling organization be made available for public scrutiny.

Failure to give adequate attention to a poll's performance has opened the door to all kinds of polls—from bubble-gum to all varieties of straw polls—with the result that the public and the press are thoroughly confused and ready to believe that "a poll is a poll."

On occasion a bubble-gum poll will be right by accident in an election and if the public hears only about this one time when it was right and not about all the other times when it was far off the mark, the public can not avoid being confused. And the same principle applies to polls that are allegedly scientific.

If the best polling procedures are followed and if those who employ them are competent, then final results arrived at during an election campaign should show a reasonably close correspondence to the official returns. This does not mean that they must be on target in every election, but certainly they should be fairly close over a number of elections.

Another cogent argument for giving proper attention to a poll's performance is to provide those in charge with an incentive to improve the poll's procedures. If poor performance is excused, overlooked, or forgotten, then there is little reason to spend a lot of money and effort on trying to be accurate with the result that shortcuts and the least expensive procedures will be substituted for better practices.

The goal of polling, as has been emphasized throughout this book, is not to "predict" elections accurately. But the elections of candidates and official referendums do provide the best testing ground for poll procedures, and offer the public the best assurances that the methodology employed in ascertaining public opinion on issues also is sound.

          o   o   o

The Nedzi hearings established the fact that constitutional law experts are extremely dubious as to whether the government can regulate polls without violating the First Amendment. Efforts by some state legislatures to prohibit poll-taking during election campaigns, to require the licensing of poll-takers, and to compel polls to reveal the names of persons interviewed, are clearly unconstitutional and almost certainly would be ruled so by the Supreme Court.

On the other hand there is less doubt that the government can legally insist upon the disclosure of polling procedures and sponsorship, since similar laws are in effect in the business and media worlds.

State laws, as pointed out earlier, can obviously apply only to those polling organizations operating within the state. The proponents of state legislation to control polls typically overlook the fact that polling organizations need not be located within a state in order to poll there. A poll of the state of California can be conducted by a polling organization located in any other state, and it can do so without having an office, or a single interviewer, in the state of California. The results of such a poll, moreover, could be published by every newspaper in California under the full protection of the right of a free press. Only Federal regulations, therefore, would be effective in this situation.

Candidates' Complaints
About Polls

Many persons in political life, and especially candidates who have been defeated for office, complain that polls "seriously distort and undermine the electoral process." It should be pointed out that this process, as presently followed, is largely of the politicians' own making and for their benefit. The electoral process was never designed explicitly to aid and abet the democratic process.

If the public had its way, the electoral process would not only be undermined, it would be altered completely, and in its place would be established a process that is less manipulated, less corrupt, more efficient, more informative, and more democratic.

The public would change every aspect of the electoral process: the way candidates are selected, the primaries, the party conventions, the length of campaigns, the conduct of campaigns, and the manner in which funds are raised to pay election costs.

Most Americans hold politics and politicians in low esteem. If proof is needed of the public's attitudes, one need look no farther than the voting turnout in national elections; more persons stay away from the polls on election day than in any other major democracy of the world.

Most politicians still believe in the bandwagon myth and ritualistically assure voters that they, or their candidates, will certainly win on election day. Because poll results often indicate the contrary, there are those who would like to see polls banned or forbidden to publish results during the last two or three weeks of a campaign.

However, the banning of election polls would still not keep voters in the dark about the way the political race is going. To achieve this goal, it would be necessary to prohibit all private and confidential polls taken by the parties or candidates and all too often "leaked" to the press by the candidate who is ahead. It would be necessary to ban the prognostications of political writers and experts, especially if they were based upon the results of private or confidential polls.

Complaints about polls, of course, go beyond the reporting of the standings in the race. David Shaw, writing in the *Los Angeles Times*, puts these complaints into three categories: money, media, morale— "the three "M's of political campaigning." Specifically, charges are made that: (1) election polls tend to dry up campaign funds for the candidate who is trailing; (2) election polls dampen the morale of campaign workers when they read poll results showing their candidate behind; and (3) election polls reduce media exposure for the losing candidate.

Each of these three charges must be examined seriously since, undeniably, they are based upon hard evidence.

THE DRYING UP OF CAMPAIGN FUNDS

Many candidates have reported that their financial support has completely stopped after poll results have shown them trailing. This points to an important and to a disturbing conclusion—that most campaign contributions, even small ones, are given to candidates not out of party loyalty but in the expectation of some kind of pay-off. A candidate who is unlikely to win is in no position to grant favors. So, here is the strongest possible argument for prohibiting all private contributions to candidates and for the government funding of political campaigns.

Perhaps what is needed today is not only a Truth in Polling Act but a Truth in Legislating Act which would require each member of Congress (or of any legislature) to report every time he casts his vote for a bill whether he has received any campaign funds or campaign help from individuals who have a personal, an organized group, or corporate interest in the bill in question.

Or maybe what is needed is a modern Martin Luther who will lead a fight for reformation in politics, inveighing against the selling of legislative indulgences to anyone who puts up enough money in political campaigns.

If the electoral process worked in an ideal manner, then, certainly, every candidate for office would have an equal chance to be elected, with the same opportunity to have his views and qualifications brought to the attention of the voting public as any other candidate despite wealth or incumbency.

Our present electoral process gives an unfair advantage to the candidate who can afford, out of his own pocket, to buy television time and newspaper space and to hire a big staff of workers. It also gives an unfair advantage to the incumbent who can, and usually does, spend a great deal of his time—and, in the case of congressmen, the time of a very large staff paid for out of government funds—to get ready for the next election almost from the day he assumes office.

To offset these advantages—to establish what might be described as an Equal Opportunity in Politics Program—many basic reforms will be needed which, unfortunately, those who have won office by the present electoral process must approve. So, that day is not likely to come very soon.

One small step in the direction of reform might be taken by adopting a practice followed by the State of Oregon, by some foreign nations, and, in fact, in some local elections, by the League of Women Voters. This is the practice of sending, to each registered voter in a given state or constituency, a brochure that describes in detail the background and qualifications of each candidate and gives each an opportunity to present his views on important issues.

THE DAMPENING OF MORALE

A poll that shows a candidate doing poorly can dampen the morale of the candidate and of his campaign workers, but it can do so *only if they have been misled into thinking that the candidate has greater political strength than, in fact, he has.*

If a candidate permits himself to believe that he is running a better race than is the case, and is shocked when he sees poll results, he has no one to blame but himself if the polling data dispel this illusion.

Common sense would dictate that a candidate should start his campaign with a fairly realistic evaluation of his chances. There are many ways of doing this. If the candidate can not afford a polling expert at least he can instruct his workers how to sound voter sentiment without going to very much expense. Even two hundred or three hundred telephone calls, properly and objectively done, will provide some indication of where the candidate stands. This type of polling will not tell him whether he is 4.4% ahead or behind his opponent, but it will tell him whether the race is fairly close, whether there is a sizeable gap between him and his opponent, whether he is far behind or far ahead.

Having assessed the situation in this manner, his strategy can be formulated accordingly. And without this kind of intelligence he is flying blind.

In case a candidate finds himself trailing in the race, there is always hope. Campaigns should never be considered lost until the votes are counted on election day. The candidate who is ahead can always make a last minute blunder (shades of "Rum, Romanism, and Rebellion"); events can always alter candidate standings as can other last-minute developments. Finally a candidate's party workers can make a real difference on election day by getting to the polls a higher percentage of their supporters than the opponent.

By obtaining knowledge of his standing and by providing proper instruction to campaign workers, a candidate, or his workers, need not suffer a dampening of morale arising from published poll results.

LOSS OF MEDIA COVERAGE

Newspapers have a constitutional right to ignore completely a political candidate, cutting him off without a single line in their news columns. They can use their best editorial talents to influence the electorate to vote against a given candidate without giving this candidate the right to answer. Newspapers can even print articles opposing a candidate based upon false evidence, provided they do so without malice. These rights are guaranteed by the First Amendment and have been upheld by the Supreme Court.

Needless to say, few, if any, newspapers follow these practices, although it is a widely accepted policy for a newspaper to try to induce voters to vote for candidates it would like to see elected.

The important point for candidates for political office to keep in mind is that news space is allocated almost entirely on the basis of reader interest. No editor is going to sit down with a ruler to measure the amount of space that one candidate receives as opposed to another. If a candidate is getting less news coverage, the likely reason is that he isn't saying or doing anything worth reporting. It is extremely unlikely that a newspaper would deliberately reduce the space given a candidate simply because he is shown to be trailing in poll ratings.

Certainly one way to get greater media coverage, and, in fact, to win campaigns, is to wage a vigorous, interesting campaign that is addressed to the voters' real concerns. And if the campaign has a little color and avoids the usual name calling and mud-slinging—the kind of political buncombe that turns people off—then the candidate need not worry too much about coverage in the media; he will get it.

The public is always eager to read or to listen to anyone who has something of importance to say, and it doesn't make any difference whether that person is high or low in poll standings.

Public Response Research

While public opinion research has sought to discover how the nation divides on important political, social, and economic issues, another type of research has sought to learn which of many proposed ways of solving problems facing the nation is most acceptable to the public.

In a speech before the annual conference of AAPOR (May, 1975), the writer suggested that the time had arrived when this latter type of research should be given its own name to distinguish it from public opinion research. He suggested the name "Public Response Research."

Briefly stated, this research seeks to gauge the public's receptivity to an idea, or to an alternative, advanced as a solution to a particular problem.

Problem solving usually begins with a search for alternatives or options. The next step is to find out, for those problems which concern legislators and administrators, which of the alternatives or options is most acceptable to the public.

This doesn't mean that policy makers must accept the alternative the public prefers; another alternative may be better. In this case, however, there is an obvious need to discover why it is less popular and what can be done to meet the public's wishes. The only reliable way that this can be achieved is by means of survey research procedures traditionally employed in gauging public opinion.

It should be borne in mind that while basic procedures are the same as those used in assessing public opinion, the objectives and mental processes involved in public response research are different. In the case of public opinion measurement, persons interviewed have typically given some thought to the issue in question; they have weighed the pros and cons and have reached a conclusion, or at least a tentative conclusion.

In the case of public response research, the proposals or alternatives are usually new to the respondent; he is unlikely to have heard their advantages or disadvantages discussed. Therefore, his choice of options requires a different kind of mental projection and weighing.

The early beginnings of this effort to discover whether a new proposal is acceptable to the public go back to the days of the "trial balloon"—a device which Presidents often used to gauge the public's reaction to a new idea.

The process was crude and usually involved a certain amount of deception. The President, or his spokesman, desiring to get some indication of the reception to a new plan of action, leaked his proposal to the press, meanwhile keeping his own connection with the idea secret. The press, in turn, gave publicity to the idea, and if it met with a bad reception—shot down, as it were—then the President could disclaim any knowledge or connection with the idea.

Survey research has put an end to this clumsy procedure. At the same time it has opened the possibility of testing any number of alternative solutions to a given problem, and in a relatively short period of time. This permits legislators and administrators to be fairly certain, in advance, that a given proposal or course of action will meet with majority approval.

An early instance of the employment of this type of research occurred in the months preceding our entrance into World War II. It will be recalled that Great Britain faced starvation unless ships could be found to guard the convoys bringing supplies. England appealed to President Roosevelt for help and a plan was born to trade destroyers for bases in the British empire.

Since the United States had not yet become involved in the war, this dramatic proposal was fraught with political dynamite. President Roosevelt, to get some indication in advance of the public's reaction, asked an early sponsor of public opinion polls, Mr. Eugene Meyer, publisher of *The Washington Post*, to ask The Gallup Poll to find out how the public would respond to this proposal. In a few days we had the results: a majority of the public approved the idea. Shortly thereafter, President Roosevelt made history with his trade of destroyers for bases declaration.

Many other similar examples could be cited. A review of the last 40 years, in the writer's opinion, would show that employment of this type of research would have enabled the nation to deal more effectively and expeditiously with many of its problems.

Specifically, as a nation we would have been better prepared for World War II; we would have prosecuted that war better; we would have adopted social reforms at least two decades earlier than we did; we would have dealt better with the problem of young persons who are out of work and out of school; we would have had less racial strife; we would have ended the war in Korea and in Vietnam earlier than we did; we would have adopted an electoral system that is far more efficient and democratic; we would have given the President item veto power that would have saved the nation billions of dollars spent on logrolling projects.

Public response research is a tool that is eminently fitted to make democratic government more efficient and more responsive to the wishes of the people.

o   o   o

It is important to identify still another type of research designed to evaluate programs that Congress or state legislative bodies have adopted. This type of assessment offers an opportunity to save the nation countless billions of dollars now spent on programs that fail to meet their intended objectives or prove ineffective and inefficient in other respects.

Many mistakes that come from ill-advised legislation could be corrected before the expenditure of huge sums of money if Congress required every new program to go through a pilot stage before it became operational throughout the nation, with careful assessment and evaluation at the pilot stage to determine its effectiveness.

This is an obvious step, and one employed by business and industry in launching new products or new programs. It is the sensible way to proceed both in government and in business.

❍   ❍   ❍

If the two types of research discussed above—the one to measure the public's acceptance in advance of a proposed program, and the second to evaluate the program once it is adopted by requiring the program to be pilot tested—were used, then virtually every government program could be assured of success, and the taxpayers of the nation could count upon the savings of billions of dollars presently spent on programs that fail in important respects or fail entirely to achieve their goal.

The Uses of Sampling Research

Appreciation of the many useful ways that sampling research can be employed at all levels of government is only now becoming apparent. During the last few years, many leading newspapers of the nation have set up their own polling organizations to be able to report the sentiment of local residents on issues that confront them and to improve the ability of local governments to deal with these.

The opportunities in urban research are many. Through sampling research it is possible to project the city's future growth or decline; to keep an annual audit of all the services provided by the city from the consumers' viewpoint; to keep a constant check on what the people regard as the city's major problems and needs; to report attitudes towards such institutions as the local public schools, the courts, the health and social services; to reveal citizens' views on taxes and where money might be saved; to express their opinion on how different groups within the city are being treated; to obtain their point of view about the businesses and industries located in the area and shopping facilities; to offer their ideas about the recreational activities and needs of the city; their ideas on crime and security and what should be done about it; and their interest in participating in local affairs.

One of the landmark surveys in public opinion research was sponsored by the Charles F. Kettering Foundation in 1975. The study, described as the "State of Mankind" survey, sought to discover the satisfactions, the hopes and worries, of people located in all parts of the world. The sampling process covered all nations of the world where public opinion research is presently conducted. Interviewing and other procedures were carried out through the facilities of Gallup International Research Institutes and embraced more than ninety per cent of the people of the world living in these nations.

The questionnaire included more than 100 items, covering not only the satisfaction of those interviewed with their jobs, their home life, their leisure pursuits, their health, their standard of living, their education, but also their satisfaction with their community and their nation.

Information not heretofore available has been obtained on the attitudes of people throughout the world about religion, about the ideal number of children in a family, about their standard of living, about the need for industry, about crime in their area, the desire to emigrate to another nation, interest in protecting wildlife, equality for women, attitudes toward and knowledge of the United Nations and the conditions of their life as related to their environment.

World-wide polling is an important way to improve communication among the people of the world, offering a mechanism to provide better information about the hopes and fears of people and the problems that confront them in their daily lives.

With better understanding should come a deeper appreciation of the desires and needs of the people who inhabit the earth, with the chances of conflict and war being reduced accordingly.

Whether a world society will develop in the future is a moot point. But certainly a world-wide poll conducted on a continuing basis would be a useful, in fact an essential, first step in that direction.

Appendix

Record of Gallup Poll Accuracy in National Elections (20 National Elections—1936 to 1974)

Year	Gallup Final Survey	Election Result°	Error on Winning Candidate, Party
	%	%	
1936	55.7 Roosevelt	62.5 Roosevelt	−6.8 Roosevelt[1]
1938	54.0 Democratic	50.8 Democratic	+3.2 Democratic
1940	52.0 Roosevelt	55.0 Roosevelt	−3.0 Roosevelt
1942	52.0 Democratic	48.0 Democratic	+4.0 Democratic[2]
1944	51.5 Roosevelt	53.3[3] Roosevelt	−1.8 Roosevelt
1946	58.0 Republican	54.3 Republican	+3.7 Republican
1948	44.5 Truman	49.9 Truman	−5.4 Truman[4]
1950	51.0 Democratic	50.3 Democratic	+0.7 Democratic
1952	51.0 Eisenhower	55.4 Eisenhower	−4.4 Eisenhower
1954	51.5 Democratic	52.7 Democratic	−1.2 Democratic
1956	59.5 Eisenhower	57.8 Eisenhower	+1.7 Eisenhower
1958	57.0 Democratic	56.5 Democratic	+0.5 Democratic
1960	51.0 Kennedy	50.1 Kennedy	+0.9 Kennedy
1962	55.5 Democratic	52.7 Democratic	+2.8 Democratic
1964	64.0 Johnson	61.3 Johnson	+2.7 Johnson
1966	52.5 Democratic	51.5 Democratic	+1.0 Democratic
1968	43.0 Nixon	43.4 Nixon	−0.4 Nixon[5]
1970	53.0 Democratic	54.3 Democratic	−1.3 Democratic
1972	62.0 Nixon	61.8 Nixon	+0.2 Nixon
1974	60.0 Democratic	58.9 Democratic	+1.1 Democratic

Average Deviation for 20 national elections, percentage points = 2.4

Average Deviation for 7 national elections 1936 through 1948, percentage points = 4.0

Average Deviation for 13 national elections since 1948, percentage points = 1.4

Average Deviation for 11 national elections since 1952, percentage points = 1.2

---

*Winning candidate or party.

[1] Average error on major party candidates = 6.6 percentage points.

[2] Final report said Democrats would win control of the House, which they did even though the Republicans won a majority of the popular vote.

[3] Civilian vote 53.3, Roosevelt soldier vote .5 = 53.8 Roosevelt. Gallup final survey based on civilian vote.

[4] Average error on major party candidates = 4.8 percentage points.

[5] Average error for Nixon, Humphrey, Wallace = 0.9

Highlights in Polling History

THE STRAW VOTE ERA

1824   The Harrisburg Pennsylvanian reported on July 24 the results of a straw poll taken in Wilmington, Delaware. The poll showed Andrew Jackson far in the lead. In August, the Raleigh Star polled several political meetings in North Carolina and also found Jackson ahead of other presidential aspirants.

1883   General Charles H. Taylor, editor of the Boston Globe, developed a system for reporting election night returns to forecast final results by sending reporters to carefully selected precincts—a system that is basically the same as that now employed by television networks to project final returns on election night.

1904   The New York Herald Tribune, a pioneer in the field of election prediction, polled 30,000 registered voters in the city of New York.

1908   The New York Herald, the Cincinnati Enquirer, the Chicago Record-Herald, and the St. Louis Republic made a forecast of the electoral college vote based chiefly on street corner polls.

1912   The New York Herald again collaborated with these newspapers and also the Boston Globe and the Los Angeles Times in a poll of 37 states, chiefly by personal canvassing.

1916   The Literary Digest conducted its first postcard poll among its subscribers in five states.

1920   This year the Literary Digest decided to mail 11,000,000 ballots to telephone owners to test sentiment on presidential hopefuls before the party conventions. In the fall campaign, a postcard poll was conducted in six states. The poll erred heavily on the Republican side.

1924   Some 16,500,000 ballots were mailed by the Literary Digest to telephone and automobile owners. This time all states in the Union were covered. The final national figure was in error by 5.1 percentage points—on the Republican side.

1928   The number of ballots sent out was again increased for the presidential election of this year. A total of 18,000,000 went to persons on the Literary Digest's mailing lists. Again GOP strength was overestimated by 4.4 percentage points. Claude Robinson recorded 85 straw polls taken during this campaign of which 6 were nation-wide in scope.

1932   All records were broken for the number of ballots mailed—20,000,000—of which some 3,-000,000 were marked and returned to the Literary Digest. This was the Digest's best year in respect to accuracy, and the only time it did not overestimate Republican strength. But part of the reason for the high level of accuracy was due to off-setting factors. The error

—0.9—was referred to as "almost magical accuracy."

THE MODERN POLLING ERA

1933   A series of experimental polls dealing with issues and politics was begun in November by George Gallup based upon two kinds of experience. In politics he had helped direct the campaign for the office of Secretary of State of Iowa of his mother-in-law, Ola Babcock Miller (the first woman and the first Democrat to win this office); in the field of research Gallup had developed and widely employed a new survey method for measuring the readership of magazines and newspapers.

1934   The first test of the Gallup polling system which was based upon small but carefully selected samples taken in areas that had accurately mirrored the shifts in political opinion in previous election years, came in the November Congressional elections. The results correctly showed the Democrats gaining seats, the first time the party in power has ever achieved this goal in this century.

1935   The Fortune Quarterly poll first appeared in the July issue of this magazine. It was conducted by Elmo Roper of the market research firm of Roper, Cherrington, and Wood. This was the beginning of the Roper poll which has had a long and distinguished record.

On October 20, the American Institute of Public Opinion, established in the Spring of 1935, released its first report to sponsoring newspapers. This poll, now known as the Gallup Poll, has reported public opinion on political, social and economic issues every week, without exception, in the forty years since this time.

1936   This year represents a turning point in polling history. The Literary Digest, employing exactly the same system as in previous elections, mailed 10,000,000 postcard ballots chiefly to persons on telephone and automobile owner lists. In their final report, the editor proudly reported that the figures were "neither weighted, adjusted, nor interpreted." Landon received 57.1 per cent of the major party vote, Roosevelt 42.9 per cent. In the election, FDR won 62.5 per cent of the major party vote. The error—19.6 percentage points—is the largest ever registered by a national poll in a presidential election.

Final figures for the new type of sampling procedures used by the Roper Poll and the Gallup Poll showed Roosevelt winning, and by a big margin. Also a new poll, conducted by Archibald Crossley for King Features, using the same scientific approach, showed Roosevelt ahead, also by a big margin.

While the Literary Digest went out of existence a short time later, it was not the inaccurate forecast of 1936 that was primarily responsible. A new kind of newsmagazine, Time, had captured the public's interest.

1937   The first issue of the Public Opinion Quarterly published under the auspices of the School of Public Affairs of Princeton University appeared in January of this year. The editor was DeWitt Clinton Poole, the managing editor, Harwood L. Childs. Associate editors were Hadley Cantril, Harold Lasswell, E. Pendelton Herring, and O. W. Riegel.

1939   Polls to test the strength of a possible presidential candidate were undertaken on a private basis for the first time. As told in his book, *All Out of Step*, Gerard B. Lambert reported: "At one time in the middle of the summer of 1939, before war broke out, my country-wide opinion polls showed Dewey leading Roosevelt by a substantial margin. The figures were not published, so few people knew about them. The war (which started September 1, 1939) changed the whole picture." In charge of these polls were two very able researchers, John Maloney and Harry Field.

1940   The first state poll, Texas Poll, was established this year, by Joe Belden, and was supported by a group of Texas newspapers.

1943   The Iowa Poll was established, the first of the public opinion polls sponsored by a single newspaper, the Des Moines Register.

1944   The establishment of the Minnesota Poll under the aegis of the Minneapolis Tribune.

1946   Publication in December of the first California Poll release, by the Mervin Field Research Corp.

1947   The American Association for Public Opinion

Research came officially into existence. The first conference of persons interested in this field had been held in Colorado the previous year. The prime mover was Harry Field, who at this time was organizer and director of the National Opinion Research Center.

1948 This was another crisis year in the history of polling. All the published polls, and all the political commentators, forecast a victory for Thomas E. Dewey over President Harry Truman. While the actual error in the poll forecasts was less than some polls had registered in the 1936 election on a state-by-state basis, when they were on the "right" side, a great furor was raised with many columnists and radio commentators happily predicting that the end had come at last for all polls.

1960 In this close race, both presidential candidates relied heavily on private poll findings—Nixon on the work of Claude Robinson of Opinion Research Corp. and Kennedy, on Louis Harris. Richard Nixon's *Six Crises* and Theodore White's *The Making of the President* describe the role played by private polls in this election.

1963 Establishment by Louis Harris of the Harris Survey, sponsored by newspapers across the nation in whose columns the Survey Reports appear.

1967 The National Council on Published Polls (NCPP) was organized to set up standards for published polls and to impose as much self-regulation as possible on polls that supply their findings to the public. Archibald Crossley was the first president. He was followed by Richard Scammon, then by Robert Bowers and more recently by Albert H. Cantril.

1970   To shed more light on what is in the minds of voters as they cast their votes on election day, National Educational Television and the Gallup Poll jointly carried out the first referendum on the chief issues debated in the mid-term elections of 1970. The Public Opinion Referendum was the result. It seems destined to become widely used as a supplementary tool to polling.

1972   Hearings on the Nedzi bill, described as a Truth in Polling Act, were held in Washington D.C. Participating in the hearings were all of the leaders in the field of public opinion research. The hearings delved into every aspect of polling and the possible influences of polling and represent the most thorough investigation of this field to date.

1975   The benefits to problem solvers and to the nation from the development of Public Response Research, as distinguished from Public Opinion Research, were outlined by George Gallup at the annual AAPOR conference.

Table of Suggested Tolerances for the Gallup Poll

The table below provides suggested sampling tolerances for Gallup Poll surveys on the basis of procedures presently in use—1976. The figures take into account the effect of the sample design upon sampling error. They show the range, plus or minus, within which results can be expected to vary with repeated samplings under exactly comparable conditions.

In Percentage Points
(at 95 in 100 confidence level)°

	1500	1000	750	600	400	200	100
Percentages near 10	2	2	3	3	4	5	7
Percentages near 20	2	3	4	4	5	7	9
Percentages near 30	3	4	4	4	6	8	10
Percentages near 40	3	4	4	5	6	8	11
Percentages near 50	3	4	4	5	6	8	11
Percentages near 60	3	4	4	5	6	8	11
Percentages near 70	3	4	4	4	6	8	10
Percentages near 80	2	3	4	4	5	7	9
Percentages near 90	2	2	3	3	4	5	7

-------------------Sample Size-------------------

°The chances are 95 in 100 that the sampling error is not larger than the figures shown.

To use the table above, these directions should be followed. Suppose a reported percentage is 33 for a group that embraces 1500 respondents. Since 33 is nearest 30 in the table, look in row 30 under the column headed 1500. The number in the table is 3, which means that the 33 per cent figure obtained in the survey is subject to a sampling error of plus or minus 3 percentage points. Another way of saying this is that very probably (95 times in 100) repeated samplings of this size would yield figures ranging between 30 and 36, with the most likely figure being the 33 per cent obtained.

It should be noted that while the largest sample in the table deals with the normal national sample unit (1500) now employed by the Gallup Poll, many surveys of this organization include a far greater number of persons, usually multiples of the 1500 unit.

Suggested Reading

GOVERNMENT AND PUBLIC OPINION

Bolling, Richard *House Out of Order,* 1965
E. P. Dutton & Co.

Clark, Senator Joseph S. *Congress: The Sapless Branch,* 1965 Harper & Row
These two books should be must reading for every student in the United States and for every citizen who is interested in how Congress actually functions. Both authors base their views on years spent in Congress, one in the Senate, the other in the House.

Bryce, James *The American Commonwealth,* 1888 and *Modern Democracies,* 1924 MacMillan
After many decades still the most perceptive and realistic account of the role of public opinion in a democracy.

deTocqueville, Alexis *Democracy in America,* 1835
Many of the weaknesses in our approach to democracy and in our election machinery, observed by deTocqueville a century and a half ago, still have not been remedied.

OBSERVATIONS ABOUT PUBLIC OPINION BASED UPON POLL FINDINGS

Bailey, Thomas A. *The Man in the Street,* 1948
The MacMillan Co.
Written when he was a professor of history at Stan-

ford University, Bailey deals with the impact of public opinion on foreign policy, meanwhile drawing many sage observations about domestic politics.

Fenton, John M. *In Your Opinion*, 1960 Little, Brown & Co.
The public's views on post-war problems between 1945 and 1960. The McCarthy era, Korea, the Catholic vote and how it would affect John Kennedy's chances in 1960.

Free and Cantril *The Political Beliefs of Americans*, 1967 Rutgers University Press
The best analysis to date of the conservative and liberal viewpoints in American politics and how these two ideologies have influenced legislation.

Gallup and Rae *The Pulse of Democracy*, 1940 Simon & Schuster
The first book to deal at length with the function of polls in a democracy, plus a review of poll findings from 1935 to 1940.

Lydgate, William *What America Thinks*, 1944 Thomas Y. Crowell
A review of the public's thinking on the important pre-war and war years, revealing how far the public was ahead of the nation's legislative leaders.

Scammon and Wattenberg *The Real Majority* 1970 Coward, McCann & Geoghegan, Inc.
A remarkably perceptive analysis of the forces at work in American politics and of present trends.

POLLING METHODS AND PROCEDURES

Cantril, Hadley *Gauging Public Opinion*, 1944 Princeton University Press
An early but still valuable book on the methods and procedures used in polling.

Childs, Harwood L. *Public Opinion*, 1964 D. Van Nostrand Co.
An excellent textbook written by one of the authorities in the field of public opinion. Probably the best bibliography extant on all aspects of this subject.

Hodder-Williams, Richard *Public Opinion Polls and British Politics*, 1970 The Camelot Press, London
A good description of British polls, their procedures and accuracy and their role today in British politics. An account of the 1970 election.

Mendelsohn and Crespi *Polls, Television, and the New Politics*, 1970 Chandler Publishing Co.
A thorough analysis of the bandwagon theory and an interesting appraisal of how television and public opinion polls are changing the political scene.

Morganstern, Oskar *On the Accuracy of Economic Observations*, 1963 Princeton University Press
A highly regarded political economist points to the dangers of accepting uncritically the published figures on unemployment, cost of living, and many other economic statistics.

Perry, Paul K. Election Survey Procedures of the Gallup Poll, Public Opinion Quarterly, Fall, 1960. Election Survey Methods Gallup Political Index, No. 7, December, 1965

Robinson, Claude E. *Straw Votes*, 1932 Columbia University Press
A complete history of straw polls conducted between 1900 and 1930. The shortcomings of straw vote methods are pointed out in detail.

STATISTICAL ASPECTS OF POLLING, PARTICULARLY THE SAMPLING PROCESS

The following books are highly recommended for those who wish to know more about sampling procedures used in surveys:

Cochran, William G. Sampling Techniques, 2nd edition, 1963 John Wiley & Sons, Inc.

Deming, W. Edwards Sample Design in Business Research, 1960 John Wiley & Sons, Inc.

Kish, Leslie Survey Sampling, 1965 John Wiley & Sons, Inc.

Stuart, A. Basic Ideas of Scientific Sampling (No. 4 in Griffin's Statistical Monographs and Courses), 1962 Hafner Publishing Co.

Yates, F. Sampling Methods for Censuses and Surveys, 3rd edition, 1960 Hafner Publishing Co.